UNCERTAIN

Entering 2020

LINDA VARSELL SMITH

ACKNOWLEDGMENTS:

Formatter and Illustrator:
Maureen Therrien Frank
TheMandalaLady.com

Information:
© Copyright 2023
ISBN: 9-781312-789937

Rainbow Communications
471 NW Hemlock Avenue
Corvallis, OR 97330

varsell4@comcast.net

Poet: Linda Varsell Smith

These poems were written during the COVID lock down. We are still emerging from masks and caution in public places, in January, 2023 as I prepare this manuscript for Maureen Frank to format and illustrate. I just kept working and dealing with seeing fewer people. Most of the writer's group kept meeting on line like: Marys Peak Poets, Children's Book Writers, Poetic License. Zoom was a new concept to grasp. The Scrabble group kept meeting with masks—sometimes in a coffee house or a home. With my husband Court, we went to the coast often so I could find new angels for my over 3200 angel collection. I also collect Swedish folk art, elves and fairies. I have seasonal creatures to shift as well.

When the weather is friendly, I like to sit in the backyard to gather chi. The weekend rides invigorate and I delight in finding new angels. Groups hopefully can gather in person soon. I do see people in my exercise class. I want to see family more. We have an adorable great-grandson who will be two in February. He is delightful. Family scattered from New Zealand to Utah. We have lived in Corvallis, Oregon since 1969. We have not regretted going West to live. Here are some of my experiences.

UNCERTAIN CONTENTS

Backyard Musings

Relating

Life During Lockdown

Encounters

Celebrations

Dreamscapes

Excursions

BACKYARD MUSINGS

Almost Touching

Early afternoon on a sunny, seventy-ish day
I went to sit in the backyard well-equipped
with watch, hat, pillow and an unused jacket.

From the jacket dangles an elf ornament from
Moon Room decorations. The sun is warm
but not uncomfortable. My fingers dangle the elf.

The two apple trees interlace branches.
The hazelnut trees stretch to each other,
but they do not touch, just shadows on lawn.

The butterflies fly right in front of me. They
explore all areas of the yard, solo or circle
dancing in the garden.

Scrub jays spread wings in the dump spot
in the garden. Today two jays social-distance
in the same area, fly away in different directions.

Butterflies and birds like the blueberry bushes.
Hummingbirds barely touch orange flower
late-bloomers. I do not see bees.

The breeze is so light Tootsie the angel weathervane
does not budge. Angel Airlika, on hazelnut branch gently
sways as if to cradle the rust, keep rust on her.

The pinwheel moves more often than the wind chimes.
The chimes do not touch very often. No dog barks for
them to keep in touch. No contrails or annoying machines.

All beings seem to not be touching. In quarantine when
we go outside or inside most wear masks outside our
bubbles. It is touching to see babies loved closely.

I grab my watch from my pocket, carry my gear inside.
I leave the pillow to sunbathe and greet me sanitized
tomorrow, when my bottom will touch its top.

2

Brief Observations

Raindrops drip
from reddened holly berries.
Drought ends.

The First Snow

Snow gloms and clumps on branches.
A few red holly berries peek through
slipped, melting snow.

The white camellia blossoms bulb,
tucked inside the branches protected
from snowy roofs.

Under the trees a circle of grass.
Snow could not filter to the ground.
But the rutted road remains white.

Later the sun comes out and I
can watch the snow tamp and dampen
the lush green lawn.

It is the day after Christmas, a belated
gift of littered snowflakes outside the window.
We have a belated white Christmas.

On Christmas the roads were clear.
We could take a tour of colorful lights
unhampered by slippery snow.

Ephemeral snow, temporary lights.
The good and bad shall pass. Footprints
in the snow will fade away.

Snowy Days

Yesterday snow-melt tears glistened
on the tip of holly leaves. Overnight we
added three inches bunching on branches.

Sun and wind flake the air and ground.
Snow globs pimple and drop clumps.
The front and back yards covered in snow.

Snow is rare in the valley so the newspaper
is filled with snow pictures and stories. People
snap photos and send them on the Internet.

I peek out windows, sit and face the backyard
with a smile. Many delays. My B-12 shot
postponed until afternoon.

As the snow melts slowly in the cold, I
check on it sporadically. A snowball fight
might be fun, but make old hands too cold.

I am content to watch and later ride to my
appointment in a wheelchair, snow slushing
from the wheels, feet held high.

Ode to Daffodils

Mid-march the daffodils burgeon
into spring. Daffodils litter lawns
in clusters, rim sidewalks.

Neighboring streets sprinkled
with daffodil patches- yellow
beacons tooting horns for spring.

We have more irises than daffodils
in our yard and they are slow to pop. I do
not want to pick daffodils, destroy their glow.

Just seeing them in our world again
is joy enough to brighten my pandemic-
punched mood. They lure me outside to see.

I am emerging from a cocoon, taking
a look around at what has changed.
The kernels of spring bring renewal.

Back to the Backyard
    March 22, 2022

The sun shines in 70's light breeze.
I am lured into the backyard to
sit and soak in spring, wearing
my new, blue soft sweatshirt.

Under the filbert tree, I see seed pods
and curled brown leaves. One pod
drapes from the arm of Anglica,
a swaying, rusty, metallic angel.

All the trees are very green-mossy and fuzzy
white lichen. Tiny buds budge for a spot.
With my return to ritual, amid skeletal branches,
I see blue sky and puffy clouds.

Two dandelions amid clusters of blue
lupin loll in the garden. The weathervane
angel, Tootsie toots her silent horn,
beside a faded blue and white pinwheel.

Transient small brown birds and larger
blue jays visit the pooping spot in the corner
of the yard. They also twitter as they
flitter to apple, cherry and filbert trees.

Planes' and traffic murmurs. Neighbor
plays "Don't go breaking my heart", soon
muffed by a miffed listener. Enough
of human intrusions, back to natural sounds.

This is the first time this year I've taken
sunglasses and my Peruvian wide- brimmed
hat into the yard. Little has changed here,
but in the world, turmoil splays on screens.

Observing nature calms jarring headlines.
My red hat— a stop light. Inside, the extra gear
gets stored. My hat hangs from the walker
with the glasses tucked in the head pocket.

Outside, on the blue table beside my chair,
Bottom, a prone, ten-inch concrete angel
waits for my next session, arms under his head
a sash strategically placed on his loins.

7

Out the Window

Out the TV room window I see bluebirds
in the holly tree and woodpeckers in
the camellia tree.

Brown and blue birds nibble red berries
and bounce branches, white petals fall.
On the flat screen a distant world.

COVID lock down encourages window-watching.
CD action more alluring. TV often violent, reveals discord.
Wars rage. The birds share space peacefully.

When the world feels dark and heavy, I
find comfort in lush green foliage, winged
creatures, maybe the occasional squirrel.

A gray squirrel climbs up and down
the trunks, leaps tree to tree, plucks
what it wants with flare.

But are any of us really carefree? How
many are aware of a imperiled planet?
Can we ever know what pulses life?

Awareness

The abundant front yard dandelions
turn into puffballs. They become
gray, see-thru, ready to blow.

No one has proven the limits
to awareness or consciousness,
so perhaps the other yellow blooms watch.

To see your yard-mates disintegrate
beside you, immobile to resist, swish
to wind-wishes, crumble...

I can foresee the process underway.
I go inside not to witness the unfolding.
The whole world is fragile. What can hold?

How long will the bright spots last?
We never had a guarantee.

Dandelion Strong

Dandelions strew across
the front and back lawns,
sticking yellow tongues at us.

They thrive despite disease
and darkness– beacons
of light–sturdy reminders.

I stare at them as I walk
indoors or peer at them through
enclosed outdoor room windows.

I have been delinquent
to sit amid them this season.
I would not need my mask.

Dandelions persist despite mowing.
Watering is discouraged
during this drought and cutbacks.

But I am drawn to them, grateful
we can water them enough
to keep them alive.

I could use their tenacity, their light.
Can I face my challenges—
dandelion strong?

I will risk going outside to sit,
as soon as I find my shoes and hat,
after I finish typing.

Sitting in the Sun
July 24th 2022

A day before our oldest son's birthday,
I lug the black wire chair from patio
to the back lawn, in a sunny spot near
the hazelnut tree.

The cherry, apple and hazelnut trees
display their green mossy patches
on their trunks and light green lichen
beards. Not sure what these growths are.

An unripe small apple falls nearby.
The blueberry and strawberry patches
conceal their treasures from me in the
stone wall crossing the yard.

We have ripe blueberries now- picked
by my gardener husband. Two pinwheels
vary their spins to suit the breeze.
Two wind chimes jangle from the roof.

A monarch butterfly flies right in front of me.
Several white butterflies or moths check
me out. A black ant with red eyes explores
my left middle finger- twice before leaving.

The weather is perfect sitting weather- mid-70's,
but it seems hotter. I did not wear my sunglasses.
My masseuse stops by with my reading glasses
I left after yesterday's massage.

Our new pinwheel has rainbow-shades blades-
three layers of them compete for speed. The brown
birds visit briefly, at a distance. The grass grows
independently of the mower at different heights.

I cheer for the escapees that survive despite our
efforts to tame them. I like a raggedy lawn.
Tomorrow I'll re-grieve our oldest son's death.
Today I'll celebrate his life.

Appearances

Appearances are deceiving.
Blue sky conceals pollution.
The air needs a refreshening.

When I sit outside to breathe
garden, backyard air, what I
cannot see still is ominous.

In public, masks are needed for
a new B strain of virus. Some
people still are oblivious.

Tomorrow we will drive to the coast.
We plan to visit a small town's craft
fair. They'd like you to wear masks.

We will as always. But I'll wonder
what lurks under the masks and what
the unmasked are spraying.

With such gorgeous, sunny, slightly
breezy weather, one can be deluded
by appearances and balmy facade.

How long will this cautionary tale last?
No one seems to know. The babies born
into such a precarious world concern me.

Masks follow me everywhere I go.
The bare-faced folk worry me more.
Around the world people live in fear.

I am 82. I had many unmasked years,
but always some disease was out to
bug-a-boo us into vigilance.

And the Heat Goes On

We are still dealing with temperatures
that are high for Oregon, part
of climate change facing everyone.

I miss communing with my backyard
in my comfortable chair under
the hazelnut tree. It squats without me.

When I have tried to sun soak, I
am very uncomfortable very quickly.
My knee miss the lower heat.

Driving the car for exercise class or
even our weekend coastal rides, I am
inside a store or see waves through windows.

Finding new angels for my collection
uplifts my spirits. I marvel at the diversity
of expression and creativity.

Inside I can sit and gaze at them. They
are in every room. Mostly I'm in pandemic
isolation. They are a pick me up.

I also have seasonal mostly Annalee creatures
on counters, tables, shelves happily grinning
at me. I put up Halloween in August.

My coven of witches smile in my bathroom,
black cats sprawl in my husband's domain.
Other rooms host Halloween hot spots.

I vary my clusters from year to year, but
the enclosed Moon Room has been Christmas
with even a wooden tree, for a few years.

I like to think they might communicate on their
own wave length and I am providing a place
to see each other, even if they are immobile.

They are my eye candy—a treat like dark
chocolate. I do not care if some think it odd.
No groups are currently meeting in homes.

My patient, mostly oblivious husband barely
notices. He just considers it clutter, no matter
what the season and shrugs.

Since childhood I have had an affinity for dolls
which are still on display and they can witness
the newcomers and their visitors.

Little great-grandson Achilles sees the low tables
covered with Halloween creatures. With a swift
swoop sends many troops toppling to the floor.

His parents are appalled as I laugh and assure
the felt figures will not break. I was less supportive
when he stuck a head in his mouth.

I do not leave anything breakable in a toddler's
path. Choking on small toys is a hazard.
But his lovable grin is a delight.

Soon I can sit outside and watch him race
around the backyard. I watch out for bees,
He will always have loving eyes following him.

As I stare out the back window, I hope to go
outside soon with a pillow for my chair and wear
a wide-brimmed hat. I have a new hat to try out

The dandelions wait for my praise—
little beacons of light in a dark time.
The backyard is my garden of delights.

Backyard Solace

After a stressful, fraudulent call from
Medicare, I retreat to the backyard
trying to calm down. I worry my numbers
have been compromised. I responded
poorly to what I think was a scam.

In a sunny spot under the hazelnut tree,
I see a squirrel scamper in the canopy.
Apples plop and hazelnuts fall. The pinwheels
intermittently whirl with wind-gusts.
Colors blur, a new one spins rainbow hues.

When my husband delivers a chicken
pot pie for lunch, my fumble fingers knock
it to the ground. It looks like vomit. I will leave
it for a squirrel or deer. Not appetizing. They
probably have standards.

The heat beats through my shirt to my back
and arms. With dark glasses, wide-brimmed hat
I return to my chair at the edge of shade.
My knees relax. But the call worries me
and I cannot relax. The scene soothes.

The pandemic has curtailed my outings.
My shingles resides in my left eye and
a sore shoulder. I am not comfortable
and after a while I quit to take a nap.
Wind chimes greet and bade farewell.

I hydrate with Bai. Inside I eat a piece
of dark chocolate fudge– much more tasty,
soothing, makes me forget aches. The birds poop
in the garden corner. Deer will gobble the apples.
Critters rustle the branches to free fruit.

I enjoy witnessing normalcy in the cycles.
On the surface nothing seems awry. But
I know the pandemic changes routines and
where I can get out of the car. But at home,
I have my garden respite to inspirit.

Wind-Pawns

White fluffy puffballs float
across the backyard. Not sure
of former host. Light and lovely
I follow their paths and smile.

The lawn is scraggly with tall
sentinels escaping the mower.
Lichen encrusts branches with
strong fuzzy grip. Green trunk moss.

The dandelions speckle and cluster–
some open and sun-bright. Two
pinwheels whirl color and blur
the petals. We are all wind-pawns.

Apple tree tosses apples to the ground.
Hazelnuts snatched by squirrels,
roaming the tree limbs. Leaves flutter
and some fall. Sunny breeze fans.

My hat fights to stay on. Short sleeves
on my sun-soaked, dry arms. The
metal chair is warming up. I plan
an hour watching the wind-commotions.

So much to ponder as I sit and contemplate
all the pandemic closures, masks... The
predictions for when this all ends is
not very optimistic–maybe never.

I am sad for the youth of the world
faced with a curbed future. The impacts
on public gatherings, schooling, things
we took for granted not so long ago.

I want to help, but feel powerless.
I may be depressed, old and hurting.
I want predictions to be healthy and
optimistic. So I sit in the sun for warmth.

Apple Picking Time

Mid-day, mid-August I sit in the backyard
slurping up some sun. After it gets too hot
I move under the shade of the hazelnut tree.

Two apples dropped as I sit. Over thirty
apples nestle into grass. I hope a friend
comes to get some for her horses.

At my feet a single seed of a puffball
struggles to free itself from a hazelnut
husk. It seem to have independent agency.

The wind aids some but it moves without
wind. I watch intrigued as it struggles to free
itself from the leaf, rays wildly flailing.

When I go inside, I pick up the seed
and blow it toward its next destination.
How will the seed get to its last landing?

The two metal angels hang facing in
the same direction, horns pointing west. I
blew the seed easterly near the patio.

I hope I helped, but I so not know a seed's
consciousness. I assume inanimates
are aware, so I treat them with respect.

One last glance as I go inside. Will I see
it tomorrow when I rescue another seed?
At least I tried to assist life.

Pondering the Pandemic

This invisible cage masks us,
exposes us to illness, coops
us inside, as summer fades into fall.

In public people are freeing their
faces–but what are they causing
to themselves and others?

Meetings are on zoom. Some
just opening up to in-person
gatherings and critiques.

I admit critiquing writing on-line
and on zoom is convenient and
comfortable, but miss in-person chats.

On our weekend drives to the coast, I
look from my wheelchair at unmasked
tourists, who feel safe for they are outside.

But inside the shops distances are not
ideal and merchandise handling– iffy and
perhaps germ transmission enhancing?

This COVID cage dampens contact,
visits, makes me worry about my
family's and friends' futures.

My great-grandson will think the Lone
Ranger and masked criminals are all
just part of the pandemic cast?

I want him to take deep breaths
and be a safe child. There always
has to be challenges in being human?

After all this time on Earth, why have
we not done better for peace and health?
I am tired of waiting for emerging hope.

Haiku Sequence

The window pane
a pointillist painting of rain
dribbles and drools

wet leaves shine
droplets bubble
then pop

white-capped waves
foam on the shore
clouds cover the sea

Uncertain weather
in uncertain times
uproots my mood

RELATING

Unlocking

Yesterday in exercise class, only I wore a mask.
My writing groups are still on Zoom.
My Scrabble group resumes at a member's
home at the end of the month.

After two years of mostly relating on screens,
I have become accustomed to communicating
in this fashion. It has allowed me to keep in contact
with Sweden, New Zealand, across the states.

When it warms up, I will into the backyard,
soak in any sun available–unmasked, alone.
Adapted rituals can return to original ones.
What is the key to this unlocking?

The key is risking contagion, even when
likelihood is low. I am cautious to keep
family safe–especially my great-grandson.
Next week we resume having family visits.

They will come in nuclear units- three batches.
We can focus on each individual better than
gathering all at once. The seasonal decorations
are St. Patrick's day- green figures on orange cloth.

Ukraine consumes the news, which is sad
for the hoped for progress of humanity.
During the pandemic, I've tried to maintain
some optimism. I've unlocked fear.

Dandelion Dancing

Our one year-old great-grandson
Achilles brings me two freshly
picked dandelions.

We each hold one, to sway
as we sing and dance. I am
stepping in my rocking chair.

He is dancing on recently
balanced, stocking feet. Our
hands free to hold dandelions.

He smiles and laughs as we
enjoy our dandelion dance
in the midst of lock down.

I put the dandelions in water
in a short jar. The next day
the dandelion heads droop.

The petals closed, Two
wilted dandelions hang over
the edge, dancing day over.

The Red Button

A red button, the size of a dime,
dangles in a white oval from my neck.
It is a life alert system for when I am alone.

My husband and I decide we should
test it before he leaves on a trip, so
I press the button.

Near the phone is the white, boxy alert
system gadget which rings. I go over
to talk to it. This is an ideal scenario.

In reality I might be plat on my stomach
or stuck like a turtle on my back. Would
I be nearby or able to get to it?

I have seen some where you talk directly
into the button which makes more sense.
Out of the house it does not work.

The front door has a lock system
which is really unhelpful, I do not
want to lock it. It has a code.

My necklace red light is a nuisance.
It is not practical for me, but hubby thinks
it a wonderful device. He does not wear one.

Will guilt make we wear it even when he's
on his trip? At massages and exercise classes
I will have to rely on associates to call in mishaps.

I look down at the keys and the red eye
stares back at me, teaches me I should not
type looking at the keys. Too late for that.

Alternative Realities

When we dream, do we go
to alternate realities we don't know?
Do we get a glimpse at another dimension
which 3-D keeps in suspension?

Many times I am in my youth,
seeing other possible truth.
I return to my childhood home.
In Connecticut I roam.

I visit angel shops in unknown places,
interact with unfamiliar faces.
I don't remember the point of the dream.
It is very elusive it would seem.

But the imagery moves me. Sometimes I weep.
Sometimes the dream wakes me from sleep.
I think I will remember when I get out of bed,
but often a dim memory is left instead.

I do not have to write it down, I think.
But the dream goes over the brink.
I remember feeling very engaged,
but the impact remains caged.

But for a while I know there is plurality
in the cosmos–we are just one reality.
Better or worse an experience than Earth?
Just keep living life and give it worth?

The End of Roe

The end to a woman's bodily autonomy.
The end to freedom of choice.
The end of women's safety and health.
Neither rape or incest is considered.
Women are victims to male lust with no justice.

I am just glad I never had to make the decision
to abort a fetus. But I would never impinge
upon the rights of another to control their fate.
And what about the children conceived and
birthed? What are both parents' responsibilities.

Are the mothers incubators to deliver babies
for adoption? Should the father be held
liable for costs for the child? If contraception
is abolished we will live in a patriarchal prison?
Both sexes have to make good decisions
about reproduction. What if they goof?

Ideally a child should be planned, wanted,
properly cared for. But reality does not
always work out that way and children
suffer. They do not even protect young girls–
molested by incest and rape. Should they
be forced to bear a child when they are a child?

Many other countries are more enlightened.
They are disillusioned about America's leadership.
They even laugh at us. But it is the children I
mourn for– thrust into a difficult start by irresponsible
parents or the mother's heartache at giving up the child.
I am so sad, brimming tears.What a disappointing world!

Breathing in a Polluted World

Poetry is a way of to remember our relationship with the natural world is reciprocal. It's having a place to breathe and having a place to pay attention.
Ada Limon- 24th US Poet Laureate

With the COVID pandemic and many in lock down.
Vaccines and masks relied on to protect us.
Political turmoil, climate upheavals,
the natural world is paved and air polluted.

When can we risk crowds? Safe guards enough?
We went to a POW Wow with very few masks.
Dazzling regalia, fascinating footwork, faces uncovered.
They danced with determination and precision.

But while I was one of the few masked folk,
I worried about my great-grandson–unmasked
and unvaccinated. He is one and still breast feeding.
I have no idea if his parents are protected.

All the chanting, singing- blowing air around!
Feet pound artificial grass in a circle.
Not a full house, but almost. We are forced
to breathe in uncertain air.

I have been avoiding crowds for months and months.
Poetry readings are returning–outside.
We have a filter on the furnace and when cooling.
I need to go back to the backyard to sit and breathe deep.

The weather is good and backyard filled with flowers—
my favorite dandelions. Will today be the day I return,
draw my attention to the outdoors rather than indoors,
and watching screens for connection?

Riding the Waves

Heat waves, COVIC, money pox,
climate changes— Earth seems
besieged by violence and fear.
Civilization rips apart at the seams.

In lock down most of the time, I
interact with screens, go on rides
enclosed in the car, to exercises
and massage. Who decides?

I wear a mask in public, many do not.
I no longer do grocery shopping
or use a sitting cart. Limit trips.
I see no signs of stopping.

I plod along with poems, chat on phone.
Computer companion at my fingertips.
Sit too much. Standing hurts knees.
I also find my memory slips.

I welcome visitors. I fawn over
my great-grandson who warms my heart
with his actions and radiant smile.
It is hard to be so far apart.

Oregon is such a beautiful place
and feels safe amid chaos, delusion.
As I age, I appreciate kindness and love
which is my wavery brain's conclusion.

Book Support

Feedback from my latest book
brought calls, cards
and unexpected gifts
of books, stuffed frogs
and a Willow Tree angel.

Readers say they like the look
of the cover and angelic guards
in the illustrations, with lifts
to the spirit and creative cogs
to leap to another angle.

The next book is "Uncertain"—
a pandemic attempt to entertain.
Word play tries to shine light,
despite a future that may not be bright.

If this book resonates
and to some communicates,
I am happy to connect.
I have curiosity to project.

Predicting the Future

Shaman, psychics, card and palm
readers, divining rods users, fortune
tellers, visionaries, with or without
tools to aid their probes— some people
claim they can see other's destinies,
some believing it is foreordained.

Some practitioners somehow prove
very accurate, some misinterpret, sometimes
we cannot cope with what they tell us.
I have met some extraordinary men and
women who were uncannily accurate. But
even forewarned I could not change fate.

Some losses were almost unbearable
and the scars are still with me. The sad
side of loving is loss and a part of me
has never recovered from the loss of our son.
We have been fortunate to have much good
in our lives as well, but the image of him haunts me.

I cannot erase that he was run over by a truck driver
as he rode his new bike in Tuscaloosa just after
his 19th birthday by a truck driver who did not ever
tell us he was sorry and he had driven over others
as well. He received no punishment. No compensation
would replace Kip for us, but his killer's no responsibility, pains.

That was 1982. I wonder how many others he has killed
with impunity. Decades have passed and with every
family birth, there is a tinge of fear for their safety. I have
learned the glean the happy times, sometimes for a few
hours, I have felt peace. Not often. I visualize his sitting up
and calling out "help me" then dying on hot Alabama asphalt.

Headlines

The newspaper headlines
tend toward dark and sadness.
Reading the newspaper can be
a real downer...tamped gladness.

People need hope, pandemic
routines to make them feel safe.
TV and media still try comedies,
but the news make nerves chafe.

I tend to shift channels of reality
toward more light-hearted fare.
No violence toward anyone. Parents
must remain diligent and aware.

I want a bright future for my family
and all the other families around the world.
I feel helpless unable to assuage
the disease, darkness that's unfurled.

Are we headed toward extinction?
Do we have much of a future left?
Have we messed up our planet,
leaving sentient beings bereft?

The warm summer sun disguises,
masks earth in green. I watch
and appreciate beauty when I can.
I hope planetary creations rematch.

Carpe Diem

I still do not understand
how we seem to stick out
like porcupine quills from
the round Earth yet appear
to be vertical.

I still do not understand
sentience and how anyone
would think the creator of the
multiverse would create such
a huge creation just for
a puny, iffy species to explore.

I still do not understand
why, if creations evolve
I see so little evidence of it.
People should be so much
more peaceful and intelligent
by now after eons of trying.

Perhaps we are on a planet
for the dregs of the universe?
We incarnate here for another
chance to make amends or heal?
I wish I understood it all to bring
more meaning and love ----if
that is the goal not suffering.

What Should I Devote My Attention to?

The newspapers, TV, computers blare
mostly negative news and events
I either do not care about or are just
unpleasant to contemplate.

Do I retreat into my imagination?
Try to ignore what I cannot change?
When do I act to support or reject? How
 do I protect vulnerable loved ones?

I am about to declare a media break.
I can write using pen and paper not
plunk keys. I can go low-tech for awhile.
Maybe take more naps?

I can delay plugging in. Concentrate
on immediate family as they struggle
with the pandemic, health and safety.
I am clueless what I can do to help.

Many countries are in the midst
of cultural shifts which disenfranchise
certain populations. Gender and political
concerns still unresolved and difficult.

As the newspaper sprawls before me,
I turn pages looking for the brightening
articles. When watching TV news they
try to end broadcasts with an uplifting tale.

How much darkness do I witness for
tidbits of light? The balance is wobbling.
I need to retreat to the backyard again
to contemplate any helpful actions.

But aging slows all parts of my body–
brain included. I do not feel as capable
of reaching out and taking a stance.
What I am devoted to requires reevaluation?

I am tired of the twaddle of the privileged like
doltish King Charles who inherits power only
because of his birth not merit. Royalty is an
expensive relic. Why are some devoted to it?

Winning the Lottery

Imagine my surprise at winning
80 million dollars in a lottery in a
dream. I have never bought
a lottery ticket, let alone win.

I had to distribute my largess.
First I gave one million to my family:
husband, son, daughter, three
grandchildren and one great-grand-son.

But I had oodles left. Should
it be two or three million each
and then give to my favorite
causes? Which ones?

Such a lump sum to one person.
I have seen this on tv and wondered
why they spent winnings as they did.
Wealth distribution in wonky.

When I woke up from my nap,
I was relieved it was not real.
I thought about what I would do
if I ever won. It is a mind game.

I am sure I would get all kinds
of advice on how to spend it.
It could be very stressful. Best
I still never buy a ticket.

An Elusive Dream

Back in graduate school my husband
worked with the Papago Reservation.
In my dream I was back in Arizona
visiting Papago.

The people were so warm and welcoming.
Especially a little boy about seven.
I felt so happy to be there walking
and talking to this child.

In an art museum there was a portrait
of an young boy. I believe the tribal name
was Seri. We could not afford to buy it,
but over 60 years later I wish we could.

This painting returned in my dream along
with an encounter with an enchanting child.
My great-grandson has a small amount
of Native American blood from his mother.

Perhaps the portrait was a foretelling
of the wonderful little boy in my future?
Images of both boys make me smile
and my heart beats with hope and love.

The Proposal

In a dream I flashback to 17.
I'm in a high school cafeteria
alone at a lunch table.
Two boys approach. One is
tall, blonde, athletic who I
name Biff as I don't know him.
The shorter dark- haired boy
I knew was named Bill.

They sit down and Bill proclaims
they had the rings and in Biff's behalf
proposed marriage. I stutter that
I hardly know Biff- even his name.
How could I marry someone I did
not know? Biff was broken-hearted.
I felt terrible and managed to squeak,
perhaps we could go out a few times
and see how it goes.

Biff and Bill fade from the scene
and I have no idea from what dimension
they are from. It looked like my high
school lunch room, but then I am not 17.
I am 82 and have no memory of such
a classmate. I do remember a Bill
that might fit that part. Memory and
dreams. How we mix up our reality!

How to Achieve Balance?

Today I received two books from a friend.
I have talked with several friends and
had a Scrabble meeting cancelled.

Today I have scoured many, many emails
which my husband feels is long overdue.
I have thousands still to delete.

Cooped up by the pandemic I find
advice from the TV, computer and
over the phone. I am still uncertain.

How do we achieve balance in such
a turbulent time? Have we learned
anything from the past chaos?

I am very sad contemplating the future
for my great-grandson. I have no idea
what he will face and how I can protect.

Vulnerability at any stage of life is painful.
I am inside too much. I do not sit outside
to sustain my chakras or any part of me.

It is too cold to sit outside in late November.
I change my collectibles for the seasons.
Pilgrims, Native Americans and turkeys–soon gone.

I am trying to get some zest and get to work
on changing these seasonal companions. But
I can fudge a few days and collect just a few more.

For all my family I will try to boost my enthusiasm
and let the holidays— on time or not– enlight my light.
We are planning for family in units this year.

It will be wonderful to see them in person,
Someday we can all be together and not worry
when we unmask. I still mask for us all.

Pandemic Pauses

Life presents daily pauses,
makes me ponder many causes.
All the viruses floating about
with all the illnesses they flout.

I fear for all whether vaxxed to the max
or doubters whose protection is lax.
Loopholes open and infect,
whether diligent or by neglect.

My great-grandson not quite two
is dependent on what others do.
Unmasked, he is vulnerable, as we
surround him with love from family.

He runs and plays— feeling fine
as we gather to chat and dine.
I hope when we leave we are safe,
but my worries continue to chafe.

He is exposed and I am fearful,
I try to be upbeat and cheerful.
Having lost a beloved son by bike accident in 1982,
it is not an experience I want them to go through.

So memories and fears haunt me today.
The sadness mixed with joy get in the way
for me to just be in the moment –at ease
when I feel engulfed by possible disease.

In the COVID Cage

When I muster energy and courage,
I break out of the isolation COVID brings
to exercise–masked.

Mid-October we went to Bauman's Harvest
Festival with grandson, his partner and
great-grandson Achilles.

Normally I'd shy from such large
public gatherings, but to see family
was a lure, not orange bubbles on ground.

Few people wore masks which worried
me, but I worried more for unmasked
great-grandson.

I look at the week meetings and all
moved to Zoom except Scrabble. I
Spend most of my time at home.

Though Achilles has not seen us too
many times, he greets us with a smile.
I do not like to think of COVID cages.

His mother and he go to the daycare
run with his mother's grandmother,
so he is very social, gaining words.

Mostly I connect by phone and computer.
Attending an in-person funeral recently
with few masks made me leery.

Despite all the shots, I feel fragile.
My enthusiasm tamped by fear.
Open the cage door–soon.

Catching Up

Each day I sit at the computer
and read news from around the world.
Much of it is dark. I yearn for light.

A line of photos indicating subjects
sprawls across the screen. I must
click to get the intentions.

Too much about the war in Ukraine
and combatants around the world.
Is there a cosmic cause for such unrest?

What vibes do we imbibe from the universe?
What is the origins of such negativity?
We must absorb this sadness from somewhere.

When I go outside, things look normal.
When we drive to the coast, the waves
still shine as they lap the shore.

Television programs still offer choices.
Newspapers dark. Turn off grim news
with a click. Turn the page.

How can we protect ourselves from
the evil of others? I can't catch up
with the news and face the day with a smile.

LIFE DURING LOCKDOWN

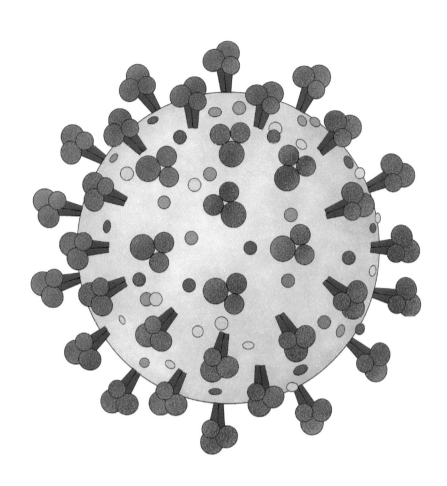

Still Masking

At the clinic patients and providers
still wear masks.
As insiders and outsiders
they do their tasks.
      Colorful masks design faces.
      Different masks for different cases.

Still wear masks
after months of quarantine.
If someone asks
I'm content not fully seen.
      A mask supposedly increases protection
      and reduces chance for COVID infection.

As insiders and outsiders
work together to mask fear,
some COVID stand-asiders
won't mask it would appear.
      They think of themselves over others.
      Their lack of responsibility bothers.

They do their tasks
with or without COVID yokes
as ignorance basks
in un-vaxed folks
      Think of babies without a vaccine chance?
      What if parents refuse to advance?

Colorful masks design faces.
What do babies think about masks when removed?
What is it a mask covers? What is it mask replaces?
Have mask reactions ever been proved?
      Does a human have this removable flap
      one can add and take off in a snap?

Different masks for different cases.
Some double up, wear a face shield.
For lookers-ons their identity erases?
Count on what the eyes yield?
      Some masks conceal facial imperfections.
      Masks provide wide selections.

Nearly Mid-July

We are in the heat wave season
without cloud-blocks, cooled
by ocean breezes in our backyard.

The floral slaughterer mowed every
dandelion, buttercup and clover head,
de-coloring lawn, curbing diversity.

He called himself a manscaper until
I told him a manscaper refers to male
grooming of his pubes and below the belt areas.

After a discussion for a better term
we agreed to primitive landscaper.
He is proud of his trimmings. I am not.

After a bike ride he intends to deflower
the front yard so he suggests I take
a look at the doomed plants before mowing.

There be dandelions! Birds pluck red
holly berries. Camellia petals fall.
"Where have all the flowers gone"?

Meanwhile under the hazelnut tree
Airlika angel has spotty rust. The
protective layer has been breached.

Soft jingle of wind chimes with gusts.
No dogs bark. Hose looped. Tootsie
weathervane angel and pinwheel dormant.

I wear my short-sleeved, red Bazinga tee shirt
for the half-hour sun-sit. Apples, hazelnuts, peaches,
plums, pears, strawberries and blueberries ripen.

Our yard is blooming on schedule. I love to escape
confinement to see nature still performing despite
wildfires, heat wave, COVID, climate change.

Bees in the grass, two blue jays in the dump spot,
butterflies flutter near me to say hi. The yard
is alive, green (grass has brown areas).

Mid-July is promising. I will choose hope.
I may risk taking off my shoes, move to shade,
tilt my hat, protecting my face in gratitude.

Pandemic Moments

Masks conceal faces
Eyes without shields unprotected
Remain six feet apart

On-line shopping
Vaccines await mandate
Some groups vulnerable

Weekend Oregon drives
Drive-thru dining
Venture into few stores

An outdoor Saturday
Market–dressed in full gear.
Soon to mover indoors.

Family gatherings held
in units of households
Whole family—not yet

Thanksgiving segmented.
Christmas still a risk?
What will new year bring?

Remembering Beauty

Poetry gives us a place to make sense out of the contradictions and the
complexity of life, a place to remember beauty. Joy Harjo

During the COVID pandemic many are isolated.
In public most wear masks to protect self and others.
We are encourage to become vaccinated.
Lock down tamps close contact. It smothers.
> We cannot walk freely in indoor places.
> We risk contagion from surfaces.

In public most wear masks to protect self and others.
Colorful designs or boring medical kind.
For some a mask is threat to freedom. It bothers
those of conservative ilk many find.
> It seems selfish to put others at risk.
> The friction between divisions are brisk.

We are encouraged to become vaccinated.
We need three shots to become most protected.
I applaud those who participated,
those who cared for others and selected,
> the hopeful tasks to avoid contagion
> for the welfare of the world— not just our nation.

Lock down tamps close contact. It smothers
urge to hug, kiss unless we know their vaccine status.
We'd like to have more contact if we had our druthers.
This is a conundrum facing all of us.
> I think of those too young or ill to mask.
> Sensible adaptations are all we can ask.

We cannot walk freely in indoor places,
dine out with drive-thrus or order in.
Be cautious of possible risky spaces.
We should be considerate of friends and kin.
> On rides I soak in Oregon's lushness from the car.,
> the beauty of green trees, rural areas from inside so far.

We risk contagion from surfaces.
when I examine angels in small shops,
on food containers there are traces.
The vigilance never stops.
> I glom onto beauty whenever I can.
> A glint of hope for any plan.

COVID Lock down Protocols

Pandemic lock down brings
lack of touch, hugs, connection
outside the home. In our cocoons
we reflect on what comes next.

Some of us do not have comfortable
situations to be cooped up in. Some
loneliness and yearning for friends
and family likely symptoms of the times.

The world is on screens. We take drives,
but stay in the car, use drive-thru
for food. We contemplate pick-up
groceries. Mask and vaccinate.

I am surrounded by 3000 angels
which I enjoy appreciating even
more than usual. I hope they help heal
my eye shingles, sore shoulder and knees.

It is cold and gray outside. My Valentines
Day decorations sprawl on tables with
red-hearted tablecloths. Red and white
accents to inspire love, lighten spirit.

Life seems in limbo, confined. Meetings
on Zoom. Will spring let us break out
like butterflies in clear, blue skies?
Where does one turn for guidance?

Smiling

A smile worms across my face
as I observe many moments
surfacing.

I smile when I find what I misplace,
clear head of negative comments
menacing.

Some people rise and some disgrace.
Some clarify arguments
resurfacing.

Fake smiles are commonplace.
Depression, predicaments
racing.

A genuine smile to interface
with all the trauma/drama,
tracing.

A smile uplifts lip curves, replacing
response to fading detriments,
embracing.

Wearing Masks

What good is it to wear face masks?
a confused public tends to ask.
Is it to protect an individual?
Is it a risk to the public overall?

Masks and vaccines keep COVID at bay
as we strive for normalcy every day?
Masks can conceal an ugly, ill face.
Exposing virus to others is a disgrace.

However

Some claim it is a matter of choices,
shout with ill-informed, self-centered voices.
Freedom to infect is not a birthright
if it increases risk to another's plight.

With colorful and medical masks I'll conform
to the new situation with a new norm.
Should I coordinate mask with outfit?
Naw, I'll do my best until I can quit.

The Naked Poet

The poet always stands naked before the world. Allen Ginsberg

Is being naked enough or is it revealed consciousness?
Being naked can expose self-serving ugliness.
Poetry just skin-deep or a revelation of insights?

Some poets want to cover-up imperfections.
At 82 I would not want to be naked in public.
Even my thoughts are filtered before on the page.

Ginsberg says "always stands naked." Really?
Many people would not notice poets dressed or not.
Many people do not read poets' exposed thoughts.

Ginsberg in "Howl" runs around naked.
I do not read much Ginsberg these days.
How much intensity and stimulation ignites me?

Will I "go gently into that good night' with Thomas?
It appears I do not have much control over my exit
or even in lock down during a pandemic.

I could walk around naked inside my home,
but it is too chilly. I prefer accouterments.
I rarely check my likeness in the mirror.

I wonder how many poets stand naked
before the world in any sense? Isolation
creates words on pages or screens.

These days I would at least need a mask
to go in public. Perhaps it would conceal
my identity if I chose to go naked in public?

No Mask Mandate Day
  March 12th 2022

Today the indoor mask mandate ends.
Driving to the coast for angels, fudge
and zippered hoodies, some people
wore masks outdoors and some
restaurants had no masks signs.

The windy, misty, sometimes rainy
shore nipped uncovered faces.
We drove to Newport, up to Lincoln
City with shops named Hippie Trick
and The Creaky Witch.

First stop was The Chocolate Frog
where we stocked up with my favorite
fudge and found two hoodies with zippers.
They will be excellent for exercise class.
My well-used sweatshirts are hard on my
well-worn sore shoulders when removed.

We are not ready yet to go unmasked
into many enclosures. Yet we did go inside
The Chocolate Frog for fantastic fudge
and two zippered hoodies. Nearby
The Christmas Shop had seven angels
ready for me to take home.

Both fudge and angels are mood-brighteners
during this lock down. Most meetings are still on
Zoom. We are resuming Scrabble in players'
homes. Writing groups retreat from Zoom
to in-person meetings. Some are hybrids.
As mandates end, choice returns.

I chose to protect myself and others with a mask.
I may return to colorful cloth masks from the
medical white masks. The fabric masks reveal
more individual expression. We must find ways
to lighten the spirit. For me the mandate does
not end now. But I'll put a more colorful face forward.

Certainly Uncertain

Lock down procedures
vary, as well as compliance.
I am often unsure how to act,
tend toward self-reliance.

I am often the only one masked
in an inside public setting.
Rules were relaxed. I
wonder what I'm getting.

Masks cover smiles, half a face.
I can not ascertain expressions.
How to act in public?
Now not only Zoom sessions.

I am not a follower if I disagree.
Should masked still be worn?
I am weighing the factors.
Where's my responsibility borne?

I wear a mask to protect others–
especially the old and young.
I don't want to cause illness.
Who am I safe among?

I restrict my outings. Isolate
the best I can.
Ponder what to do,
what's the best plan?

With spring, life flourishes—
unseen a new variant breaks through.
How will this influence others,
dictate what I can't do?

Public Masking

Masking guidelines get fuzzier.
Some people risk no masks in public.
We went to Portland Art Museum
to see Frida Kahlo and Diego Rivera.
The crowds were mask- mixed. We were
among the maskers.

Our guest also wore a mask.
The three of us dodged clotted groups
before the paintings. Six-feet apart
did not happen. We had two vaccines
and two boosters. They were old, perhaps?
I get out so seldom these days.

I mask at the market, massage, doctor
and exercise classes. People vary on
what they want to do for protection.
We have so little control over this pandemic.
Babies must be puzzled by the masks.
Some faces are colorful art minis.

At the moment I am wearing the k2 mask-
boring white. But lurking in my drawer are
the fabric masks, waiting until I gather
courage to wear them–an element of danger.
I did wear them at first until urged to protect
others I am in contract with better.

Mostly I remain in my home-cocoon and watch
lives on screens. Screens can be turned off,
but masks in public might be awhile until retired.
There are flu and shingles threats as well. I've
had shingles and the shots. At 80 I've probably
had most flus. Masks will be my bandaid from germs.

COVID Cage

In exercise class I am the only one masked.
At massage I also wear a mask.
Except on weekend rides, I stay home.

We did go to see Rent in Portland.
We were masked, some weren't.
My face is semi-protected and colorful.

Some young children see all the masks
and wonder why adults wear them.
They can't understand a free face.

Despite having all the shots, people
are still contracting COVID. Nowhere
is safe–especially in public.

I think of my great-grandson and
his enchanting smile. He is a year old
and I have not seen him masked–yet.

I feel confined. I am waiting for warmer
weather to go sit in the backyard to
contemplate the world– alone.

But for now I connect by computer
and phone. Few visitors. I would
love to hug my family–but out of reach.

How long until the COVID cage door opens?
When will this perilous passage end?
I am not a patient person...but I wait.

Outside the Window

Sun sparkles on the leaves
of the holly and camellia trees.
Butterflies and bugs land
to nip or rest. Wind shuffles branches.

I enjoy the window screen just a glance
away from the more diverse tv.
Something about the year round green
brings comfort in the pandemic.

The shades stay up until night
brings a chill. With no sun, the leaves
are shadows, just waiting for shine
and warmth. I wait eagerly.

Kindness

During lock down for the pandemic,
I limit my exposure in public places.
I am vaccinated and masked, but cautious.

Some groups still meet on Zoom.
Others brave outside meetings.
Visits less frequent–screens and phones.

Emily made a surprise visit, carrying a small
bucket of chocolate ganache. She remembered
I was diabetic and reduced the sugar.

The pail will be wonderful to play with when
emptied. My great-grandson can fill it
with sand, food–fun. But I'll nibble slowly.

He is coming to visit today. We will go to
the Saturday Market with him and his parents.
Then we will have a salmon dinner here.

The pail is on the TV table. A spoonful whenever
I choose. Kindnesses like this make lock down
lighter. I had given her my latest book.

She brought me a treat in a dark time. I'll
take dark in chocolate any time. When I pass
the pail on–what should I fill it with?

Heat Wave Singes

Too hot to sit outside and roast—
94 and deep heat sun, kept
me inside. I set up Halloween.

Usually I wait until August to
take down spring and put up
Halloween. But I was ready.

Since I ditched exercise class–knees
and because of heat. I wear masks
in public everywhere. Mask-less I set up.

The spring boxes fill up and the Halloween
boxes empty. I love the witches, cats,
pumpkins- especially the witches.

My Annalee felt angels with winsome
faces make the creatures, lovable,
not scary. That's why I collect them.

Few people will be coming to see them
with meetings now on Zoom. I hope
family in groups can come over soon.

4th of July figures came down as well.
Now the tablecloths, benches, bathrooms
are refurbished...joyful, spooky fun.

On the toilet top in my husband's throne,
I put a collection of cats. On mine I have
crone witches which make me smile.

I can leave them up until Thanksgiving.
Christmas decor in the outdoor Moon room.
Pick your holidays—or enjoy them all.

Heat Waivers

Linn and Benton counties
have not been as hot
as other Oregon counties.

Governor Kate Brown issued
a state of emergency for most
of Oregon.

"due to extreme high temperatures
causing a threat to life, health
and infrastructure."

Linn and Benton counties were
the only two counties not included
in the declaration.

My husband bikes early in the morning
before heat rises more, but it does not
cool off that much at night.

The Department of Emergency Services
Coordination Center will provide essential
protective measures to local government agencies.

People are urged to drink plenty of liquids,
go to cooling centers and check on neighbors,
friends and loved ones.

They should list these centers which will operate
24/7 during the heat wave. They say visit their
website, but again don't tell us how.

At least we are not Texas. The poor have few
protections from heat. Not much shade. States
vary in their services. AC units go to some.

I will try to help as I can, for I love Oregon and
in all areas want Oregon to thrive. Hope to see
toasty friends and family soon- as things cool off.

Coping With COVID

COVID precautions keep me mostly
housebound, except for exercise classes.
One Friday massage and my social calendar
fills up. I re-started sitting outside.

Masking up for meetings postponed.
Zoom meetings preferred. Haircut
done at home. White hair falls on floor
and into grass. Can't cut hair masked.

Now we have some B strain. Still need
shot for shingles as well. When will
the pokes end? I feel like a pin cushion.
My arm is sore. I feel achy.

Everyone copes the best they can.
Some ignore masking and shots.
I peck away at keys in my COVID
cocoon. Next book adds poems most days.

My left eye still irritated from shingles.
This sounds so whiney. My angel collection
and weekend rides keeps me hopeful.
Oregon in summer is gorgeous.

Everything looks so normal on the surface.
But hidden forces diminish our thriving.
My great- grandson sees many half-face
people. Some masks medicinal—others colorful.

Family visits less frequent and friends
on screens and phone. Dark chocolate
helps lift my mood. COVID cages are
everywhere, heeded by some.

My pain is physical and mental. Sometimes
I am at the verge of tears. Words liberate
my spirit–even if no one hears or reads them.
I am moderately coping with COVID – sadly.

The Times They are A-Changing

Pandemics, political upheavals—
nothing seems predictable, perhaps
nothing ever was, we just hoped.

The pandemic still masks us in public—
if we are diligent and want to decrease
disease. Many go out bare-faced.

I can only try to protect myself as many
feel the threats are over and disregard
warnings to public safety.

I have curbed my excursions. Weekend
drives are mostly in car en route. I mask
when going in a store. Dining is drive-thru.

We prepare for elections with some
extreme candidates and dubious promises.
Oregon is mostly center- ground?

Masks conceal emotions- mask for good
like the Lone Ranger or bad like bandits.
I don't affiliate.

I wish there was more I could do to help.
The future is so uncertain and ominous
for my great-grandson.

If I were child-bearing age, would I risk
bringing a child into these conditions? Would
I have enough hope for humanity to try?

Pondering the Pandemic

This invisible cage masks us,
exposes us to illness, coops
us inside, as summer fades into fall.

In public people are freeing their
faces—but what are they causing
to themselves and others?

Meetings are on zoom. Some
just opening up to in-person
gatherings and critiques.

I admit critiquing writing on-line
and on zoom is convenient and
comfortable, but miss in-person chats.

On our weekend drives to the coast, I
look from my wheelchair at unmasked
tourists, who feel safe for they are outside.

But inside the shops distances are not
ideal and merchandise handling- iffy and
perhaps germ transmission enhancing?

This COVID cage dampens contact,
visits, makes me worry about my
family's and friends' futures.

My great-grandson will think the Lone
Ranger and masked criminals are all
just part of the pandemic cast?

I want him to take deep breaths
and be a safe child. There always
has to be challenges in being human?

After all this time on Earth, why have
we not done better for peace and health?
I am tired of waiting for emerging hope.

Pandemic Probes

Activities curbed by pandemic precautions,
I find myself attending few meetings not on
Zoom. I just go masked to exercise classes.

We went to the Fall Festival for arts and crafts.
Many unmasked people crowded the booths.
My wheelchair gave me close views.

We were two of few masked customers of few
masked vendors. I managed to find three angels
for my collection and a small felt owl.

Perhaps it was an unnecessary risk to go,
but it was outdoors on a sunny, warm day.
I thrive on the creativity and discoveries.

I saw a friend from a pandemic-paused
group we both miss attending. We pondered
if we could get the group together soon.

We need to go to a funeral in California
in a few weeks for a college friend of my husband,
who was a fraternity brother.

We will be masked despite what others do.
We have our shots, so we are not lethal to others.
The weather deceives us that all is well.

I worry most about my toddler great-grandson
who lives in a closed up world full of masks—
Lone Rangers? What are they concealing?

He sees half-faces and only eyes. He is
too young to wear masks at his Mom's
preschool. He has beguiling, happy smiles.

I pull down my masks to peek-a-boo with him.
I want him to see my full face and delighted
smile. He lights up my world with hope.

Word Weary

Words gush from the TV,
splatter across the newspaper,
leap from the page.

Words emerge from a peck
on my computer keys, guide
my thoughts, grab my attention.

When I nap, I hope for silence
from words. Even my brain seeks a break.
I feel overwhelmed by events.

How do I respond, create from chaos?
Dreams so far seem to return me
to my late teens and college days.

Words grind the thought-bits
and spit them out in some form.
Will my hesitant breath stop breathing?

During the pandemic I am masked,
so words struggle to escape
through flimsy fabric.

So much to process everywhere.
Sitting in the backyard is too chilly
and unappealing at the moment.

Tomorrow I will emerge in public to
play Scrabble, masked in a restaurant.
Is it worth the risk? Are masks enough?

I will find out tomorrow and hope for the best.
For so long my words have been caged. I yearn
to be with other word weary, word fans.

The Hospital Triad

The Unexpected Visitation -1

Still weathering inside from a light snow storm
amid a pandemic after an appointment
shift and new directions, my confusing
ride is I somewhat warmer and balmier.

Mid-week we arrived at the clinic early for my
physical–delayed a few weeks due to
the doctor's issues. After I got
processed in immediate care, she was gone.

After tests, I learned I was being committed
to unit 4 room 3111-2— a merry-go-round of
medical staff. I donned my bare-assed gown.
My blood sugars were out of control.

My Very-Medicated Companion- 2

A thin sheet of fabric fenced Gena and me apart.
She received shots in clusters every few hours.
She was in great pain. The shots increased
her misery. She asked a care-giver if she was snappish.

Gena the TV blasting day and night. I slept in patches.
Across the hall was a shriveled old crone who
looked like Baba Yaga the witch with her coven of family
and friends visiting. Her hospital socks wiggled free from covers.

The medical staff wore beautiful royal blue uniforms- one nurse
added snowmen and Disney characters. All professional
and polite. They would adjust bedding, change inclines,
turn TV (a pod on a stalk) to the volume I wanted, give meds.

Food was adequate, many unsalted choices rather
tasteless. A dietitian informed me I had to make better
food choices to improve. I walked with walker better
than they expected and my grip was very strong for 82.

I took it as a vacation- no responsibilities except to
do what they say. I was not in pain except for injections.
They were confused for a long time. Finally they decided
I need meds adjustment and to see a diabetes educator.

Going Home

I am a letter not a number fan, so all the numbers
they were so concerned about were a mystery
of meaning. Finally 105 blood and I could go home.
My haphazard blood draws need revision.

On my husband's earlier visit he brought my supplies
to leave. At first 1 was the time to go, but I was home about 11:30.
My husband and son were watching the World Cup.
My son saw parts of several games before he left for work.

When he left at 1 I took a nap for a long noiseless nap.
I was a movie cowgirl like Ginger Rogers. I was middle-aged
and fit–riding the range. It seemed an odd transformation
as I am not into westerns. Last night it was cold and

slippery out , but now it is warming and perhaps we and go
on a ride to the coast. Things can return better normal if
I am diligent. Hope my role as a fuzzy gray-haired potentially
dementia patient is over. I can hope.

I pondered many decisions past and to come in the hospital.
How can I be more creatively helpful? With a sore big toe,
shoulders and knees, I hope to hop-a-long with as few meds
as possible and be grateful for supporters.

Snow in the Mid-Willamette Valley
     Our First Snowfall   November 6, 2022

Peering out the window,
snowflakes fall on the ground
and melt. The ground is too warm.

Some snowflakes seem
to hold on to each other
into a snow clump.

All afternoon snowflakes
make their brief appearance–
unexpected.

We did not plan on going out
today, so we can relax and
enjoy the snowflakes fall.

Warm inside, I sense the chill
outside. I wonder at the varying
size of the flakes.

If I caught one could I see
their unique design? Snowflakes
dampen the earth, uplift spirits.

It is getting dark. I have a hard
time seeing them. But it is comforting
they may blanket us through the night.

Living with Uncertainty

Should we still wear a mask in public?
Any meetings we can attend without masks?
How long will this confinement last?

Must we keep people at a distance?
Can we hug loved ones without fear?
How can we express love?

The world impinges from newspapers
and TV screens. We read and watch.
How can we help? What can we change?

The children are placed in peril
without protections. Can they be
educated in safety?

We try to keep up with suggested precautions.
We do not want to make loved ones ill.
We miss certain meetings in person.

I am trying to cope, feeling little control
over my encounters. I yearn to meet
openly without masks. Soon?

Living with uncertainty means being
cautious. Make sure you act as
responsibly as you can.

Many people are a violent threat.
The pandemic is an invisible threat.
Many confused and ill folk threaten us.

At the moment I do not feel hopeful,
despite the enticing weather. I worry
about family and friends.

I need a soothing break. Some time
to relax in a safe place without demands.
All this uncertainty is draining.

Masking Up

In the clinic waiting room,
masked patients sit patiently.
Most masks are white or black.
Some are light blue.

One woman had a colorfully
designed mask. I commented
to my husband, I wanted to get
some colorful masks.

The kind lady handed me a mask
like hers and said they were giving
them out at the clinic at another
location. I thanked her.

I exchanged my blank white mask
for the new one. It was not as
protective as my medical mask,
but it was more cheerful.

All the people sat, quietly muffled.
A young black track star wore a
black mask – not a Long Ranger,
but local high school athlete.

Halloween is a few days way.
I can pretend we are masked
for that occasion. A few coughs
are captured by the masks.

How long will we see half-faces?
Public faces covered. Young
children must be puzzled and get
confused. Do they know someone?

Under masks are grimaces and grins.
We express our emotions with our faces.
Blank stares? Caging our faces makes me
sad. When will I breathe freely in polluted air?

CREATIVE ENCOUNTERS

Instant Fire

At an unknown time in another dimension,
my cousin Karen is young and alive.
We walk to a middle school to meet friends.

We were staying in a travel trailer nearby-
like on vacation as there was no school
in session.

A firebolt enflames the trailer we left
recently as well as a restaurant. A huge
black cloud roils the sky.

We run to check damage when the fire
stops— without any intervention. The trailer
and restaurant are in tact. Nothing burned
and no people were injured.

We ask the customers in the restaurant
what had happened. They say they
are safe and I should record it.

So I record the dream, despite
being confused about the message.
I puzzle possible symbolism.

I get up to write this down,
then go back to bed. Maybe I'd
get some answers if there are any.

I can't ask Karen unless in a dream.
What instant fire causes no harm?
Certainly not in Ukraine.

I can not go back to sleep. Before
breakfast, I write this down and hope
for no fires anywhere.

Great Mysteries

There cannot be only one path toward such a great mystery. Symmachus

So many theories, settled for beliefs.
Must we choose one path to anything?
So many questions. Diverse answers.
What if we have not discovered
the data we need for an informed choice?

Ambiguity and uncertainty cloud my judgment
but I am not inclined to decide anyway.
I look for new ponderings and expressions.
Mysteries can remain mysteries. Poetry
approaches expand and provide options.

Creativity encourages exploration,
adventurous thought and actions.
Some past paths lead to violence,
conformity, false allegiances. Now
old, I cast off what I found untrue for me.

I welcome freedom of choice as long
as it does not impinge on the rights
of others. The world has too many
bullies and deceptive leaders. Followers
beware. Keep on your own selected oath.

Frida...A Self Portrait
>Portland Center Stage
>Written and Performed by Vanessa Severo

>*I never paint dreams or nightmares, I paint my own reality.* Frida Kahlo
>55 of 143 paintings are self-portraits.

The first play at the theater in 18 months.
Audience had to show vaccination cards
and wear masks to attend. Everyone did.
I had a face shield because I was to be
in the front row in my wheelchair. But
I was too low to see the stage and moved
to the back row where I had a panoramic view.

Frida is a Mexican painter. Her father German
and her mother half-Spanish-Amerindian.
She married Diego Rivera an ugly, fat, nasty
man who she married twice. She had polio
at six and walked with a limp. An accident
left her in great pain for the rest of her life.
They indicated she died at 47 from the drugs
she took to alleviate her suffering.

No matter what afflicted her she painted.
In her hospital bed for many surgeries,
at her home called Casa Azul, on travels.
She showed the world her truth, her vulnerability,
and her humanity.That was a revolutionary act.
Joanne Schultz

Three clotheslines crossed the stage. Clothes
representing various stages of her life hung
on the line. Even a pillow and blanket. Vanessa
wore several of them. Two baby clothes indicated
miscarriages. Very effective and powerful staging.

I learned of Frida while an editor at Calyx.
We featured her in an issue. Her long skirts,
colorful outfits, flowers in her hair portrayed
in photos and paintings were haunting. So
when I had the chance to see the play, I was
eager. I joined the standing ovations. To know
oneself is an important and illusive goal. Frida
did it. If she could do it, despite her perpetual
pain perhaps I should try.

We Went to See Rent
    Portland Center Stage   June 16, 2022

We head for Portland to see the musical Rent.
In the lobby we see a man with rainbow colors
in his curly shoulder length hair.
I tell him I like his hair and he thanked me.

I did not know it was Will Wilhelm who
plays a touching, poignant Angel.
We had front row seats so I could see
his facial expressions. Very intense.

Will was so convincing. I still see him/her
days later ending on a hospital bed,
dying of Aids. In the program
bio Will is called they/them.

Will is part of an excellent cast, but
his portrayal resonated with me most.
My grand-motherly instincts kicked in.
The sense of peril makes us all vulnerable.

The threat could be COVID now–spreading
to anyone despite gender and orientation.
AIDS is not obliterated. The play is a reminder
to treat everyone with kindness and compassion.

Headlines

The newspaper headlines
tend toward dark and sadness.
Reading the newspaper can be
a real downer...tamped gladness.

People need hope, pandemic
routines to make them feel safe.
TV and media still try comedies,
but the news make nerves chafe.

I tend to shift channels of reality
toward more light-hearted fare.
No violence toward anyone. Parents
must remain diligent and aware.

I want a bright future for my family
and all the other families around the world.
I feel helpless unable to assuage
the disease, darkness that's unfurled.

Are we headed toward extinction?
Do we have much of a future left?
Have we messed up our planet,
leaving sentient beings bereft?

The warm summer sun disguises,
masks earth in green. I watch
and appreciate beauty when I can.
I hope planetary creations rematch.

Einar

In the back of a classroom
I met a starving poet prototype
in a tall, skinny, shaggy black-haired
man who that day was calling
himself Einar.

He changed his name often,
sometimes daily which made
locating him difficult. I walked
to a blackboard in the front
of the room.

On the chalk rail was the cover
of his poetry book. It was a colorful,
busy design. Lots of reds
and yellows, but I could not
detect any words.

When I turned around to ask
him the title of the book, he
was gone. I woke up in my bed,
not in a classroom wondering
if I would see Einar again.

Where is Einar? In a dream
dimension, an alternative reality?
Why would I dream of this dark
poet with a bright book cover?
What is he calling himself now?

Inventing Poetry Forms

Poets and wordies love to invent
new forms to corral their wild thoughts.
I have collected several books on forms
and compiled several myself. You never
know what a poem needs.

I tend toward syllabic forms. I enjoy
rhyme. But most of my poems are
free verse- many not appearing
very poetic. More prosetry. My
ideas resist restraints.

I have many references if I want
to word play. The more forms
you know–greater possibilities.
So far this poem refuses to shape
into any poetic framework.

I opened "Poetluck" to Butterfly Form
by Michael Degenhat. Syllable count:
5-4-3-2-2-2-3-4-5. Rhymed or unrhymed.
Any subject. No stanza limit. But
instead I will invent another form-

a Lindy Loo: I am 82 so I will divide
my age into 82 words. I am too lazy
today to mess with syllables. I will
see what emerges.

Wishful Thinking

5   I wish a better future
5   for my great-grandson Achilles:
5   a name that conveys strength:
5   an uncommon name for today.

5   I wish for better future
5   prospects for the planet plagued
5   by pollution, disease, possibly extinction:
5   a lifeless, lightless cosmic ball?

5   I wish for better future
5   dreams that when fulfilled enhance
5   create a sustainable, creative existence.
5   Find a positive environmental attitude?

5   I wish for better future
5   cosmic connections with any life forms:
5   inanimate or animate anywhere. Can we
5   manifest our best intentions always?

2   Enjoy peace?

CELEBRATIONS

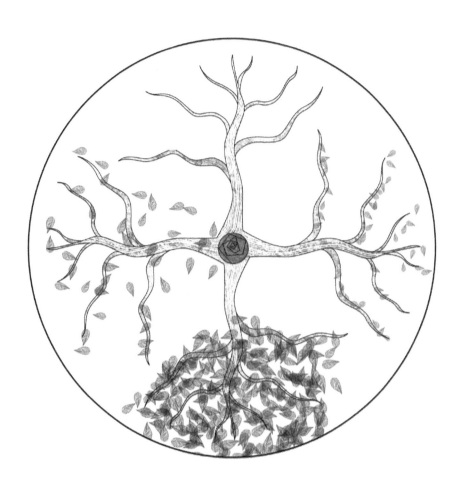

The Fourth of July 2021

Late morning it is in the 80's
with more heat wave temperatures
expected later this blue, cloudless, day.

I sit outside in my "Get off the page
and onto the stage" tee shirt, pondering
what I'll write today to start a new book.

Hazelnut tree shade spangles
my body with a hot spot on my
right shoulder. I'm speckled and hot.

Butterflies and birds fly-by. Uncertain-
to-me trajectories. Four birdsongs
heard in distant canopies.

They seek yards without pesticides,
no air pollution from fires and fireworks.
Later the valley could be smoky.

Tonight fireworks across the nation
will splinter light and boom. Scared
pets hide and seek comfort.

COVID and wildfires add to the uncertainty.
People protest. This uncertain celebration
for freedom faces many challenges.

Trauma drains spirits. Some people ready
to explode like fireworks. Parades amid
marches. I plan to stay home, mend.

E-Z Orchard Pumpkin Patch

Unexpected long line to the first pumpkin patch
we headed for, where we were to meet
grandson, his partner and great-grandson —great match,
we were delighted to greet.
       We drove to a smaller patch–still crowded to see.
       But this patch was a fun place to be.

We headed for where we were to meet
our family and roam among, find a pumpkin?
Multi-colored pumpkins and a hay ride complete
music, food in jails, saloons. Our kin
       explored in a stroller and wheelchair
       to see all the attractions there.

Grandson, partner and great-grandson– great match
a young family on a Saturday outing
Grandparents also great-grandparents watch
little Achilles who displays no pouting.
       He is amazingly good natured, didn't cry.
       Bright-eyed, curious, eager to try.

We were delighted to greet
The mother Deserie and father James.
Gatherings with them is a treat.
To keep in touch is one of our aims.
       Much loved Achilles is loving and so adorable,
       he makes the world seem less deplorable.

We drove to a small patch-still crowded to see.
We had to wear a mask to enter.
Not all masks stayed on–but most on fortunately
as there were many folks to encounter.
       The ground rather bumpy- hard to roll
       on such rough ground. Took its toll.

But this patch was a fun place to be.
Pumpkins piled to move in wheelbarrows.
We hope to go to another patch eventually.
The window of opportunity narrows.
       These perfect blue skies will not last.
       The autumnal chill is coming fast.

Giving Thanks for 2021

A year of COVID, climate change,
wildfires, political unrest, high profile
trials breeds a feeling of uncertainty,
but one can be grateful for what seems
to bring joy, happiness, connection.

Wild turkeys strut through neighborhoods.
We have seen them in our backyard and
strutting down the street with puffed plumage.
We have a small turkey for two today
as other family units meet on separate dates.

Our surfaces display felt-figures of turkeys,
pumpkins, Pilgrims and Native Americans.
All are smiling as if unaware of their fate.
The dining table will have holiday decorations
watching us eat our feasts.

I am not into the traditional holiday. We have
family members with Native American heritage
who do not celebrate the holiday. Others
explore Friendsgiving or are just grateful for
the harvest and our temporary safety.

The world faces many challenges: pain,
disruption, violence, illness, isolation. When
we eat our special meal, it will be more for
tradition and hope for a more tranquil future. We can
honor the positive progress of their descendants.

The Spiral Dowel Tree

While decorating our hanging, spiral
dowel tree with over 100 handmade
wooden ornaments, a young deer
drifted into our backyard.

We have a high fence around the yard
and on both sides we have gates. It was
a surprise to see the doe. We do get
a few each year, but the gates were closed.

Once the doe stared at me through
the large windows of the enclosed
outdoor room. My hubby went outside
to open the west gate for her.

A squirrel scampered along the fence.
The doe crossed the yard to the east gate.
She leapt over the fence as he opened
it for her. She was so agile, smooth, silky.

We resumed putting up ornaments made
by family members over the years— my parents
my brother Bob and me. The least skilled is me.
Now all three are gone, but their art survives.

The clean lines of the dowel limbs present
each ornament clearly as they spiral around
the core. I have sometimes left the tree
up for years. As I age my adeptness declines.

In the midst of the pandemic the tree represents
happy memories. Somehow even in sadness
the treasured tree uplifts spirits. I wonder how
long I will leave it up this time?

Changing Seasonal Decorations

It takes hours and hours to put
up Christmas and take down
Thanksgiving decorations but
these ornaments and figurines I own—
      colorful and uplifting art.
      Each piece is part of my heart.

Up Christmas and take down
turkeys, indigenous people and colonists.
I dislike what happened, my beliefs overthrown
for this fanciful event with lingering twists.
      Part of our country's shameful past.
      How long will mismanagement last?

Thanksgiving decorations, but
more playful depictions of participants.
Placement because I am in a rut?
I continue my disapproval rants.
      Our country has a violent story–
      lifting exploitation to glory.

Ornaments and figurines I own–
thousands of angels seasonal folks–
bring light and love to our home
and a few awareness pokes.
      During lock down I am surrounded by delight.
      I stare at my collections engulfing my sight.

Colorful and uplifting art
greet me room to room.
I don't feel so set apart.
They make me feel more welcome.
      I still collect more angels and stuffed figures.
      Their light and whimsy still allures.

Each piece is a part of my heart.
When I must leave them, go way.
I hope someone will love them, when I part
and with someone their essence will stay.
      But for now when visitors come to see me,
      they can encounter their spirits joyfully.

Holiday Lights

Holiday light bulbs bloom in the night.
Colorful lights line roofs, windows, doors.
Snowmen, angels, reindeer, Santas delight.
Decorated Christmas trees seen indoors.
> The gray skies lighten, fogs disperse.
> uplifting spirits to better from worse.

Colorful lights line roofs, windows, doors
outlining the home, displaying hope.
We drive by like moths drawn to light, car explores
displays, expanding our scope.
> Eyes dazzle as we peer through glass.
> Scenes untouchable, alas.

Snowmen, angels, reindeer, Santas delight.
Lighted by night, clearly seen by day,
Chilled by cold, but in the car quite
warm, gliding by as if in a sleigh.
> Creative ideas of holiday season—
> imagination is the reason.

Decorated Christmas trees seen indoors,
framed by windows, a back-lighted vignette.
with animals, cartoon and seasonal figures, outdoors.
This holiday season is underway, yet,
> each week more places decorate.
> More surprises. We must wait.

The gray skies lighten, fogs disperse,
even through rain, perhaps snow—
the weather conditions diverse.
But we can find joy–we know
> by taking a walk, or a ride
> as we brighten up inside.

Uplifting spirits to better from worse
of challenges from lock downs and health.
We go forth and try to immerse
ourselves in the season and by stealth,
> to find promise of happiness and love,
> with images of light below and above.

Browsing the Holiday Card List

Our newsletter says Season's Greetings
for family, friends and colleagues
as they celebrate different traditions.
M indicates mailing. E is for emailing.
Most cards are from us as a couple.
Some are from each other us gathered
from various times in our lives: childhood,
college, graduate school, places we
have lived, groups we attend.

As I peruse the list various memories
emerge, as I insert the letter in an envelope.
Now the daunting task to send emails with
an attachment. My tech skills are limited.
We both wrote the newsletter, but we rely
on him to format it. We cull some names
and add some each year. The deceased
number rises each year and are remembered.

Some of the memories are laced with sadness.
The deceased are still listed. Many have faced
tragic challenges. During the lock down from
the pandemic, many are isolated. Winter fogs
the lights. We do not have much snow in the valley.
But as we mail the letters, black ice coats the roads
and sidewalks. Ice needs to be scraped from cars.
Much connection is from Zoom. We can safely
critique writing, participate in meetings.

As cards continue to arrive, we can see how many
cope with the new nearly normal. Masks prevail.
Vaccines required many places. In a few days
I get my third. My husband has had three when
he hauls these letters to the post office. Now I
wait for my latest book copies to arrive. They are
late. Many task delays. Dreams postponed.
Worries uptake. So much unsaid in this holiday
letter as we lust for light amid looming darkness.

Martin Luther King Jr. Day 2022

On this brumous day in lock down
from COVID threat, we do not gather
to celebrate this day. We huddle
in our homes and watch screen events.

Here we wear masks in public
and order groceries for pick up.
We limit exposure by not dining out.
We must entertain ourselves at home.

We zoom meetings, chat on phone.
Cell phones have perks for some.
I am tech deficient and rely on old
technology. Few appointments.

I try to stay informed, creative, but
I am less productive since I do not
feel well due to sore shoulders and knees
plus shingles in my left eye.

I enjoy conversations in any media.
I try to be reflective and progressive.
My optimism is tarnished–gleams less bright.
I find myself worrying about others' safety.

I glean joy from friends and family.
I see people rising above gloom and
finding ways to reach out to support
others. I must polish my optimism.

Groundhog Day

Groundhog Phil saw his shadow.
Six more weeks of winter outside.
Guess lock down will be chilly.
We will be glad to be inside.

COVID closures limit our options.
Masks conceal half our faces.
Heavy duty masks preferred,
when we are in public places.

Maybe masked balls will make a comeback—
dancing away through these troubled times?
But many are hesitant about group gatherings
as the COVID death count climbs.

Poets left to explore their reflections,
and experiences from former situations.
Everyone is more introspective,
choosing from many persuasions

My fingers type on a broken keyboard.
My delete button does not delete.
All the shenanigans I go through,
to accomplish this simple fete.

My angel collection uplifts my heavy soul.
I roam room to room buoyed by their wings.
I can retreat amid their nourishing spirits.
and cope with what COVID culture brings.

Emergence

For Easter one family branch resurrects
an Easter party with bulging baskets
for children and abundant buffet.

We gathered in a backyard– the great-
grandparents of the youngest attendee
wore masks. Most did not.

No talk of the pandemic or the new surge. One
guest in a pink, bunny suit. The unmasked children
chased and wrestled, jumped on a trampoline.

We sat on plastic chairs and watched the action.
Everyone is relaxed and parents vigilant. It
could have been a past party.

For many years we hosted all branches of the family.
I loved filling baskets, Easter/spring decor. Few
see the decorations in lock down.

The family is spreading. A grandson in New Zealand.
Grand-daughter leaving for another city there in May.
COVID concerns keep us isolated.

But to see some family members was a start. Another
grandson had to work. Driving to and fro, blurs of
yellow daffodils and forsythia. Spring blooms hope.

Unhappy Fourth of July 2022

No Happy Fourth of July this year.
Limited independence, pandemic of fear.
Decoding gunshots from fireworks when
facing bullets from demented young men.

We have more guns than people in the USA.
Why does it have to be this way?
Why do we need guns in places where we live?
How many more innocent lives will be lost? Forgive?

Is the wiring defective in these killers?
Caught up in deadly destructive thrillers?
How many seemingly normal youth
run amuck, share a deadly truth?

Why are weapons of war in civilian hands?
Why can't we impose universal gun bans?
Less feeling of freedom and safety, not sure
how much longer humanity will endure.

We seem on a path of planetary destruction?
Who is leading this lethal introduction?
Death hit Hyde Park this time,
killing 7 people in their prime.

The coward dressed as a woman to escape,
as police scoured the lethal landscape.
I'm sad for my descendants- great-grandson.
Has the downward spiral just begun?

Why can't humanity improve? Seek peace?
When will the gruesome grip release?
I am overwhelmingly sad
on a holiday I should feel glad.

I am so tired to hear of a new deadly drama
leading to such terrible trauma.
Families, hopes, dreams torn asunder.
Any possibility of healing, I wonder?

Scandinavian Festival
    Junction City August 13, 2022

Despite the pandemic and no mask
requirement, we went to my favorite
event. I love the food, crafts, designs.

I traveled in style in my wheelchair,
comfortable in the warm sun. I had
to have meatballs and pastries.

I noticed a split crowd — some masked
and too many not. I worried about
the unprotected children.

We were masked as we always are
in public. Now a new strain to guard
against. Perhaps people are tired.

Perhaps they wanted to feel free,
remember the past. Despite obstacles
the festival goes on and uplifts spirits.

We are all vaxxed, masked, as protected
as is possible, but as I rode along, I
felt vulnerable and sad for the situation.

I will by-pass some festivals this year
and risk only for my favorites. I witness
the ethnic clothing, vibrant colors–smile.

I think of my Swedish relatives and wish
them well–as well as everyone everywhere.
My soul and compassion warm me up.

Sad Fortieth Anniversary

In two days it will be 40 years
since we lost our son Kip in
a bike/truck accident in Tuscaloosa,
Alabama. He was 19 on a National
a Student Exchange for his sophomore
year at the University of Oregon.

When my husband and I returned
from the coast, a friend who was
caring for our other two children
had the task to tell us Kip had died.
The university did not wait to tell us in person.
The children were in shock as we became.

I have never recovered from the loss.
I carry an innate sadness. For 40 years
my light has dimmed. At times tears flow.
I never forget for very long, even when
working on a poem. As this anniversary
approaches, the memories flow, pain intensifies.

Can I philosophize the reasons this happened
to him? Did he ever have the chance to avoid
this fate? How much is fore-destined? Did
I some how know this would happen and agree?
Did I agree to help him finish his destiny? I will
never know and never stop grieving.

He had his new bike which was shipped and
he had just picked it up. I am starting to cry
again. Was there nothing I could do to prevent
this? The truck driver did not even get a ticket.
Here it is 40 years later and the sorrow never
goes away. It is engraved in my soul.

When to Celebrate

Will it ever to safe to celebrate?
What public events should I risk?
I worry about the young children
without protections. I mask,
but it that enough?

All these viruses keep coming.
How do I love without hugs, yet
if I hug I could harm someone?
How much contact is safe? Any?
So much is unknown.

A birthday party, a gymnastics meet.
I already gave up Portland plays
for this year. Should I forgo more?
I'm 82. I can go anytime. But I do not
want to cause anyone else to leave.

How can I help young children thrive?
Will parents be fearful for years?
Thoughts and bodies are polluted.
How do we sift and sort to select
a healthy path for all?

I will not live long enough to see
my great-grandson grow up. I
just want him to have a future
that can fulfill his dreams. I
vacillate daily on the possibilities.

Preparing for Halloween

We have face-painted pumpkins
lined up to greet costumed
trick or treaters.

We do not cut up pumpkins,
but have found whimsical
painted pumpkins.

They will face off with our guests.
Our entry is well-lighted. They
should feel welcomed.

In plastic pumpkins we have
M@Ms, Snickers and Dots.
Usually we buy candy we like.

Somehow my husband bought
Dots. I'll stick to the chocolate
leftovers, if there are any.

In a pandemic, there is no way
to guess who might brave
this spooky eve. Last year–few.

Getting up and down on my cranky
knees does not sound appealing.
We will have to perfect a method.

But we will somehow see the children
get some candy–some whimsy, carefree,
sugar-loaded delights in this dark time.

Layering

Light snow lands on leaves
and earth, then melts. The snow
layer is very transient.

As rain covers holly berries,
the berries drip drops and
the leaves shine.

Rain pings on the skylights.
Drops dribble and run.
Pocked glass dims view.

Today is foggy and dry
some of the time. The layers
peel, release moisture.

The Thanksgiving decorations
have layers of turkeys, Pilgrims,
and Native Americans.

My sweatshirt is worn inside and
outside. Outside I add a jacket–
sometimes I sweat.

Surfaces moisten. Dust clings.
What layers need adding?
Which layers need discarding?

My comfort is not the only consideration.
Demands on environment–ground and air
also need to be considered.

Dwelling in watery soup or drying
like a prune, layering deals with all.
Today is a sweatshirt day.

Seasonal Transition

Haul out the Thanksgiving boxes
and empty Halloween containers
it is time to make the transition.

Tenderly, one by one I place
the Halloween witches, black cats
and pumpkins to rest in a box.

I empty the Thanksgiving gang
of Pilgrims, Native Americans
and turkeys out into the open.

Everywhere I look I can see
the new creatures and smile.
I hope Halloween creatures hibernate.

I do not see why inanimates
can't communicate just because
they lack flesh. Maybe own network?

So I respect all my collectibles
no matter the season— smile
at them and hope they feel freer.

When family comes down for the holidays,
I am looking forward to toddler
great-grandson to swish them to the floor.

They will not break and the jumble after as
he tries to pick them up as parents command.
I leave them in new tumbled position he creates.

When he leaves, I make them more orderly.
But I grin with all the memories and
visual delights they bring.

In the Pumpkin Patch
   Bauman's Harvest Festival
   Gervais, Oregon

Mid-October we head to the pumpkin patch
with crafts and food booths, tone of hay bales—
some rolls have end faces like painted pumpkins.
Most pumpkins wait the fate of their buyer.

Many pumpkins have painted on faces.
I found a very quirky uncut, but painted
pumpkin for our table...on display.
Never will eat it or make it pie.

A small creche with very simple
folk art faces also lured me in. Too
early for Christmas decor, but this
will be a beacon to the season.

We had our grandson's family with us.
Adorable Achilles and I rolled on wheels-
he a stroller and me a wheelchair.
He climbed in and out to see the sights.

It was a bumpy ride—ruts and gravel.
Lots of human obstacles to get around.
Returning this year after pandemic closures
must have brought the cooped-up crowds.

Everyone was smiling, helpful with doors
for us. A very pleasant vibe. Relaxing.
A treat for children and adults. A blue-
skied, warm day added to ambiance.

Should I name my pumpkin? I'll
wait and see what name comes to me.
To go to a pumpkin patch with loved ones,
will warm my heart for many days.

DREAMSCAPES

Shifting Consciousness

Apparently there is sleeping, dreaming
waking and cosmic consciousness.
In the dream state I visit various dimensions
and time travel. All alert states are vivid.

Last night I was lost in New York City.
On a skate board I followed a parade.
I am young. Details blur, but overall I
went to a large estate and visited a garden.

A politician (looked something like Chris
Cuomo) helped me locate my parents.
My father was in bad shape. The garden
was at the edge of a cliff, but lush.

For some reason I could not find the skateboard.
My parents had a car and we left the scene.
Many dreams I am lost. I am young and
vigorous with people I love, but they have left.

The dreams fade quickly. But for a while
I can see loved ones again. Why are most
in urban settings, lots of elevators, and
of people dwelling in another plane?

Angel Shopper

Awake or asleep I shop for angels.
I scour stores with an eye for angels.
I find newcomers for my collection of angels.

Now over three thousand angels hang out
on shelves and walls. Dangling from strings they hang out
over a table. A room we call heaven is their hangout.

I gaze at them dwelling in other rooms as well.
I admire halos, diverse gowns and wings as well.
They exude an uplifting spirit as well.

I have played an angel in youthful childhood plays.
I wrote and drew them as a child. My imagination plays
with their essence. They are part of me. My soul plays

with the concept of angels whether real or not.
I believe in them whether they are real or not.
It does not matter to me if they are real or not.

In dreams I wake up empty-handed, but I know
for a while I inhabit a consciousness and I know
angels are everywhere for me. Somehow, I know.

The Cookie Stand

In a dream I conjure
a cookie stand in the front yard
where I can give free
cookies to passers-by.

Near the sidewalk, a three-sided
structure with roof and walls
match the gray and forest green
of the house decked with a counter.

There is a chair to sit on
between customers. I buy
delicious and nutritious cookies
since I am not a baker.

Our street is a walkway for
elementary school students
to their homes and older students
to go to bus stops at the school.

Perhaps I would need a space
heater on cold, damp days.
The cookies should be in enclosed
jars to not get stale or wet.

But in my dream, shelves beneath
the counter hold trays of uncovered
cookies. I must expect a rapid turnover.
Would I compose poems or read in slow times?

But now the schools are closed due
to the pandemic. As the weather gets
chilly and rainy, few walkers pass by.
My cookie stand dream crumbles.

Shopping for Angels

This dream is different.
It seems to take place
in this dimension–earthly plane.

The gift shop looks like
a coastal location. Angels
of many media, are available here.

Usually my dream angel shops have
glowing replicas–some animated. But
this shop appears accessible, ordinary.

Some angels are made from dough art,
glass, wood, metals. Some elaborate
and some simple. I gather my choices.

An old man lets me put my selections
on the counter as I shop. Wings
and halos pile in an angel mound.

I feel it is possible to take these angels
home and not lose them when waking.
It feels so real and tangible.

These days, my angel shopping is mostly
in one shop near Lincoln City. The one place
I will mask up and go inside.

I scout for angels amid the many miniatures-
ornaments and figurines. I have yet to come
home empty-handed or disappointed.

Thousands of angels surround me at home.
They nourish my starving spirit and uplift
my sapped soul. I cherish them.

Whenever we drive to the coast, I hope
shops with angels are not in lock down.
My muse needs wings and halo headlights.

Labyrinths of Lost

In maze of dreams, a consistent theme
is being lost in a city with many buildings.
I am not old. Mostly late teens.
Am I navigating adolescence?

I worked Saturdays and summers at
a department store in Hartford,
where I was a contingent. I went
to departments that needed extra help.

My usual haunts were the smoke shop
and linens. In the smoke shop were
two elderly bachelors who were very
protective of me and patient.

I would lecture customers on the dangers
of smoking. Smoking to me is smelly
and a waste of money. The addicted
customers probably were amused by my zeal.

One customer was a deluded novelist
who gave me his manuscript to read
and never picked it up. I do not remember
where it is. Hopefully returned to the store.

While in college, I worked there summers only.
I gave campus tours during the school year.
I have fond memories of the two old codgers,
dead for decades. Now I am older than they were.

Names of all these men have faded. Mr. Shumway,
was the short, plump one. The tall, thin one
and the novelist names are now lost in the labyrinth
of memory. Poof like smoke...gone.

Lost

Since our son Kip died at 19
in a bike-truck accident in
Tuscaloosa while on a student
exchange, I have dreamed
alternate scenarios.

Last night he sat in the backyard
beside a small tree trunk which
sprouted yellow flowers from
the stump. I went to join him.

He said he had gone to Connecticut
where he married and had two daughters
named Marianna and Julie. He worked
at a wearying job. Very heavy hard work.

He had died back there while still young.
He did not say why he went to live there
to start a new life without telling us where
he was. Perhaps he reincarnated there?

Grieving imagines other possibilities
to cope with the an unimaginable reality.
It has been 40 years and I really cannot deal
with the loss or understand why it happened.

Over the years various psychics suggest
various reasons. One said Kip thanked us
from beyond for giving him the chance to live
out his karma. He was sorry he hurt us.

The box with his mementoes plus a newsreel
about his death was taken from storage. I know
who took it and know it will not be returned.
I believe it is lost, just like our beloved son.

During COVID lock down, I have plenty of time
to re-access and reflect on many decisions
and difficult situations I have faced. In dreams
I am often lost. Seeing Kip in a dream boosts
hope of reunion somewhere and acute sadness.

Dreaming

When we dream do we access
another dimension? An alternative life?
Who is writing the scripts?

Some dreams fade upon waking.
Some linger for hours before departing.
Some vivid dreams impact our decisions.

Lately living in a COVID cage, mostly
in lock down, I dream variations
of being lost in past and present.

Are we cosmic starseeds? Dwelling
in various dimensions and realities?
Do they overlap? How long do we do this?

If we reincarnate, my consciousness
could have experienced numerous lives
on various planets and universes.

As I child I imagined many beings
in many unknown locations. I crayoned
them and stapled the pages into books.

Now into my 80's I am still curious about
what's it all about. I still have no answers.
I am full of questions. Will I ever know?

Now I am concerned for future generations
having a good life, free of many perils. I wish
I could be optimistic. Too many challenges?

I gaze at my great-grandson and wonder
what his future portends. Did we ever know
our destinies? I don't know mine.

Two Snakes and a Kitten

Two snakish creatures slithered
into my dream. From under
the floorboard of a car, the first
snake emerged- a white snake
with a bulbous, gargoyle head
attached to a filament body.

The second snake had a slim,
long body with a beige, tiger head.
They stared at each other and
disappeared under the floorboard.
I have no ideas what the images
mean. They did not seem aggressive.

Meanwhile outside the car was
a hungry kitten which I determined
needed help. So I fed the kitten.
These animals crawling in my mind,
some omens? Expressions of
my concerns during this pandemic?

Upon waking I can still see them
though they have vanished. The kitten
was speckled white, black and gray.
I have no pets. More likely to find
a pet kitten than reptilian creatures.
Maybe I seek comfort over fear?

The Shortcut

A young child of six or seven
rides a red skateboard to school.
To avoid a several block route
she decides to take a diagonal
shortcut to get home.

She goes through the backdoor
and out the front door of a
stranger's home being sure
she shouts " It's me" to let
the owner know she's not a robber.

One day an elderly woman confronted
her. She was a white-haired, short woman,
plump and friendly named Paula Paulson.
They exchanged information and I woke up.
Which of them could represent me?

During the pandemic the characters would
wear masks and have spent some time out
of school. This seemed set in an earlier time
and felt like Connecticut. Paula's chubby face
and squat stature reminded me of my grandmas.

I will ponder this imagery for a while.
Who is this bold child and warm grandma?
What would I do if a child skateboarded
through my home? Surrounded by my 3000
angel collection, would I feel safe and protected?

A Birthday Visitation

Our deceased son Kip appeared
in a dream on my 82nd birthday.
He looked 19 and I was 42, like
in 1982, the year he died.

Much of our conversation is a blur,
but I remember he said he was
back for a job in Guatemala.
I was so happy to see him.

He visits infrequently and he is in
different locations. Today it was my
childhood home in Connecticut, current
home in Oregon and an unknown home.

When I awake, the grief returns and
I yearn for the dream and face
a sad reality without him. During this
COVID lockdown, I could use a visit.

A Green Snake Dream

I was at my mother's childhood
home–a large Victorian, when
I encounter a thin, green snake
with bulbous blue eyes. It is
a small snake–about 18 inches.
I manage to avoid being bit.
We are in the den, near the entry.
I am relieved as it slithers away
down the front steps.

I look up the meaning of a green
snake in a dream. I am surprised
there is an interpretation. It means
hope, luck, prosperity, joy, a new
beginning and do not give up. I
will overcome difficulties.

In the dream I feel young. So is
it for another time? I wake up
with several maladies and my
husband is on a trip. I hope
the dream portends healing. But
my body has not received the message.
Perhaps my massage later, will
bring some relief. Somehow I recall
the snake being cut up, but reassembling.
It is all a tad vague. But the huge blue
eyes with gold flecks are just dazzling.

Walking Newborns

In the dream, two newborns,
newly dressed, ask
their mothers to let
them down to walk.

In the dream two newborns
wear white, long pants.
I do not remember shoes,
but their short white jackets.

In the dream two newborns,
a girl and a boy, are able
to walk without assistance,
babble simple sentences.

I ponder the symbolism.
I had watched a documentary,
on mostly Chinese adoptions
of babies destined to leave China.

I ponder the symbolism
of making it difficult for adoptees
to discover their birth families.
Still reunions do occur.

I ponder the symbolism
of a one-child, later two child policy'
impact on families and the world.
The child is treasured.

Responsible reproduction is
a valid concern for all nations.
Mandated or not, parents should
contemplate the child's future options.

Responsible reproduction is
a needed planetary goals if
Earth is to remain viable and
pollution kept in check.

Responsible reproduction is
a possible dream? Or symbolic?
My husband says I had a similar dream,
but with one precocious newborn.

Somehow I do not remember this
recent dream, only this two-child
version. Is this a cosmic update
or a symbolic yearning dream.

Somehow I do not remember this
as representing me or my kin.
These dream mothers are part
of a global conundrum?

Somehow I do not remember this
confining of choices reflecting what
was what mothers want, but an
economic and male directive.

Early Morning Dreaming

I'm in an angel shop amid
thousands of diverse angels
made of many materials
and by delightful imagination.

I pile up my selections in
my arms , smiling at my
unearthly choices available
only in my dream world.

I am blissful, captivated,
full of wonder. Then a leg
cramp brings me back to
painful reality.

My husband brings me salted
water to relieve the cramp.
Recent mass shooting,
COVID concerns return.

It is warm under the blanket.
The shade darkens the window.
I don't want to leave my dream world
for a risky, sad, disappointing day.

Talking Baby 2

In my dream I hold a baby girl.
Her head rests on my shoulder.
Her frizzy light brown hair juts out
as if she had been electrocuted.

She has been recently born.
She says she was very excited
to been out and be able
to start her life. A lovely smile.

I am unsure who birthed her.
I remember the phrase
"Nearly seventy" but forget
the context or meaning.

My other talking baby dream
was a little boy with dark hair.
I always wondered what babies
think before they can speak.

With the pandemic, many babies
are not seeing much of the world.
When they can come out of their
cocoon, what will they say?

As I read the headlines of mass shootings,
diseases, crazy leaders and crazed
followers, babies could be traumatized
and stunned into silence.

Angelic Adjustments

Apparently my previous guardian angel
was "sacked". A new guardian
was appointed.

Apparently we do not get just one
guardian angel and some are
incompetent–flawed like charges.

No reason given for why she was
replaced. I believe my first angel
was female named Bella.

Her full name was Gabriella.
I called her Bella. The new one appears
to be male. Gabriel or Gabe?

Poor angel gets a 82 year old crone.
Does he heal, guide, ever intervene?
Guess I'll have to wait and see.

If this is true, is he a precursor of death?
Getting me ready to transition?
A comforter in my old age?

Why did she leave me? Given
a younger soul? I can just thank her
and wish her well.

I have no idea if this is truth or fantasy.
Bella and Gabe could be wish fulfillments
and hopeful dreams. Who knows?

But it is fun to think it is true and I
collect thousands of angels because
the diversity of creativity is uplifting.

Somehow all my life I have had
an affinity for angels and believe
they help me cope and hope.

The headlines are horrific and sad.
Pandemics, mass shootings, unrest.
Humanity in turmoil. Send in the angels!

Land of Nod

In a dream I visited the sleepy Land of Nod.
Princess Dawn and Prince Dusk reigned
over this peaceful place.

Early to bed, early to rise
left citizens refreshed and wise.
Early, less surly.

Not a wreck over high tech.
Avoid darkness. Line with light.
Things tend to go all right.

These goals seem hard to achieve.
Perhaps too strict to believe?
Alas, it is a fantasy.

There are gaps in this dream memory.
What remnants remain in me?
Poof. I wake up.

Collaboration

In a dream, in New York City
a young writer Rebecca meets
a young artist Robert Shuler.
The details are lost in the dream fog.

They decide to collaborate
and create a book together.
Then the dream fades and I don't
know if they made it happen.

How can such a vivid dream
just poof when waking? How
can a reality seem so real, but
is just imaginary?

Perhaps I am just in another
dream which poofs at death
or enters Akashic records,
frees from this existence to somewhere?

Is this all I get, so make the most of it?
Am I like Rebecca this time without
a clue about what is to come and what
I will create and with whom?

How much control do I have about
what I receive and create? Is there
an underlying purpose and meaning
to this consciousness?

I wake up and Rebecca and Robert
become evaporating figments of my
imagination. Are they what I wish
my life was meant to be?

My Dream Teacher

In a dream I was in a class
of a new teacher. I came
back to say good-bye

It was the last day and she had left.
On each desk was a pile of papers–
articles she wanted us to read.

There was one other student still
there who told me this young, tall, thin
brunette teacher returned home.

I had mentored this teacher. But
somehow I was late. I missed her
leaving. I was very sad.

In graduate school Dr. Marie Hughes
was my favorite teacher, but she
was old. She taught creativity.

My least favorite teacher was a man
who kept my project and never made
an attempt to return it.

This dream did not look like me, but
felt like me. In a dream reality I morph
into another version of me

I looked at the leftovers to compile
a complete set. The pile on my desk
was incomplete. This dream teacher–not me?

Mourning Mom

Over the years I have mourned
parents, grandparents, friends,
but since our son died I have
never been the same or stopped
mourning all that could have been.

It is now over 50 years. He'd
be in his sixties, but still in my
heart and mind he is 19 riding
his brand new bike down
a street in Tuscaloosa, Alabama

In my dreams he never went
on a National Student Exchange,
but stayed at the University of Oregon.
I can't see him aging, can't touch him.
He used to hug me. He loved me.

Memories are not enough. There
is always this wound, this pain,
I am never free from grief. A heavy
cape surrounds me, yet I feel cold.
There is a sadness that won't heal.

There are other children, grand-children
and even a great-grandchild to love,
but no one can replace another—just
compensate a little perhaps? Every day
I do not trust the world to be fair.

I find it hard to be in an unjust world
that allow innocents to be slaughtered.
I watch Ukraine suffer. But Russian
parents must suffer also—caught in
a conflict they had no say in.

Somewhere in the universe is there
a place I could find peace and fairness?
Do we continue to incarnate in places
where our sentience experiences sorrow?
What is the reason to live? What meaning?

The Game

In a dream, the family is eating
around a long narrow table.
I remember we said we would
go to grand-daughter Rowan's game.

Around nine of us pile into two vehicles.
I drive an old huge red truck.
It has numerous levers and I am
very uncertain how to drive it.

By some miracle we get to the end
of a water polo match. Rowan
emerges, dripping wet to thank
us for coming.

I was hoping someone would
volunteer to drive the truck home
as it was a miracle we made
it to the game.

Lost in the fuzz of the dream,
I do not know which team won
or if someone rescued me to drive
the monstrous truck home.

Not going to guess the meaning
of this dream. These are uncertain
times and strange things happen
in reality and dreams.

EXCURSIONS

Ride Detour

Our intention was to go west to the sea.
From Newport to Tillamook to home, but
by time we reach next town Philomath
we could not ignore something was awry
in our blue Fit like metal scraping road.

In Philomath he checks the tires
and looks under the car. He did not
detect anything out of place. The car
could go backwards, but still complains
going forward. Time for a detour.

We decided to go north to Monmouth.
We hit a bump and something fell off
and stopped the grumbling. Still we do
not trust True Blue to go to the coast
and we'd be stranded for a few days.

We drive by farms, forests, wineries,
Queen Anne's Lace roadsides, rows
and rows of hay in different stages
of harvesting. Some before raking,
others baled. Warm under clear skies.

Detours in Monmouth and Independence—
well-maintained charming small towns
Monmouth with hanging petunia baskets.
Independence has diverse, colorful banners
hanging from black, lantern posts.

We discuss if climate change brings more
smoky wildfires to the valley, if we should
move. We could not think of anywhere better.
I would not abandon Oregon for a few weeks
of smoke. We have air-conditioning.

We supposedly opened up July 1st. We will
remain masked in public and hope the variant
is compliant with our vaccines. Until we feel
it is safe, we will stay in the car and watch
the scenery flow like a film over our verdant valley.

Blue Valley Sky to Foggy Coast

Such a lovely fall day for a ride.
We went to Newport. South to
fudge shops? Or North for angels.

We have gone for rides to coast
often and visit Christmas Cottage
which hosts angels year-round.

This trip I found two Jim Shore angels
which are very lovely and creative. At
home I found one was a twin to one I had.

Now we will try to exchange second at
next coastal ride. Guess I am still fuzzy
from shingles meds. I am improving.

Leaves were turning en route. Few
political signs left. Still lushly green
forests for long stretches.

Perhaps we should have stayed
in the sunny valley. But regardless
of weather the sea is alluring.

Between buildings and park areas,
we see the sea's frothy waves
hit rock and sand.

Many shops are freshly painted
and appear more colorful. We did
not stop, but our drive-by enjoyable.

Despite pandemic, some tourists
were not masked. We ate drive-thru
and did not get out of the car.

I hope soon I can go inside shops
and walk the beach unmasked. Now
the time does not feel right.

Along the Rusty Road

Driving north to Astoria
through many miles
of farms and forests,
golden leaves dance
in car-breeze, slither
up the windshield, splat flat
on asphalt under blue
sky and chill-warming sun.
Orange, red, beige leaves
rust into autumn.

This day before Halloween
costumed trick or treaters
roam the streets of Astoria,
stop at stores giving candy.
Staff come to the door to
dole out goodies.

We stop at the Maritime Museum
where masks are required for entry.
Josephson"s Smoked Fish serves
masked customers. We dine on thick
clam chowder in the parking lot.
With all the colorful masks, Halloween
could be extended for months.

The hilly town of the Goonies' and
Flavel houses, founded by Scandinavians,
had no craft shops left after lock down.
I found many wooden figures there in the past.
We did find some Danish pastries

My red cape flares like a fall leaf
on my shoulders. This autumnal day
along the Columbia River and the sea
adapts to the pandemic and provides
a outlet for all the masked and cooped
up people.

Lost in the Forest Primeval

From valley fog, over the coastal mountains,
through dense forests, to sunny sea—
our Sunday ride passes through a variety
of road conditions from shallow gravel to asphalt,
road stripes by shadow and sun. Douglas fir,
evergreens and deciduous trees line
the mostly rural, cracked and pot-holed road.
It is a bumpy ride over poorly-signed territory.

We pass hunters clumped on the side of the road
around a campfire near parked trucks. We make several
wrong choices. GPS Samantha and a cell phone
seem to lack helpful directions. We confront
intersections and make intuitive choices, try
to choose roads that might head down the mountain.
Rust-colored needles on asphalt clear ruts for wheels.
My facial shingles add additional pain and confusion.

This ride was supposed to be an excursion to distract
my attention toward the beauty of nature and when
we reach the coast, soothe with a fudge shop. But
when lost, Oregon's endless green for miles and miles,
and several hours of not knowing where to go left me
on edge. The COVID pandemic kept November traffic
lighter and many stores closed. We did not know what
coastal conditions would greet us...if we ever arrived there.

It becomes sunnier as we approached the ocean.
Seagulls swirl, waves crash against rocks, tsunami signs
warn and suggest evacuation routes. We do not
get out of the car and dine with drive-thru. I toss some
french fries to three very distinctive sea gulls. One
had a mottled gray breast, white beak. Stunning markings.
I stare at them, wishing I had ordered large fries. But
I should have brought with me more appropriate fare.

We drive home in the sun on well-known roads.
We re-enter valley fog. Familiar sights calm
my agitated body and soul. Uncertainty should be
expected in these pandemic times, but I do not
feel the need to get lost and add anxiety no matter
how lovely the scenery. My beloved Oregon brings
hope there are green, thriving places in this uncertain
world. Wildfires, logging threats keep us vigilant.

Surprise Encounters

Driving to the coast amid fog
and rain, leaves and needles
line the road.

A crow pecks a dead wild turkey.
A bloody carcass bleeds on asphalt,
a heap of bones,

The coast fog obscures the sea
even when near the road. Seagulls
thrust against headwinds.

Homes' Halloween decor morphs into
Christmas. Colorful holidays perk up
the gray skies. Fresh paint brightens.

At a Christmas shop we had a
delightful unplanned encounter
with great-grandson and his parents.

His eyes dart from family to the displays
of Christmas decorations–myriad shapes
and hues. He enjoys prep for his first Christmas.

I find a Swedish looking, blonde, blue-eyed
angel ornament. In another shop I discover
a gnome with a knitted hat.

Masks cover faces. Traffic moderate. Shorter
lines at drive-thrus than expected. In this
uncertain time, so few things are surprising.

Getting COVID Shots

Shots 1 and 2 were under the bleachers
of the stadium at Oregon State in February.
Very cold, but very airy.

Today we walked into a vacant outlet store
revamped to give out shots. We had our
cards ready. About ten tables for two.

Two to a table with a wooden divider
in the middle. No one was on the other side.
Just me getting shot three.

A nurse, perhaps, administered the shots,
going table to table with a smile to pick up
paperwork left on the table and inject shot.

Since I was still recovering from shingles
on my left face, I was not eager to add
more discomfort in my arm.

But I wanted to protect others as well
as myself. Less possibility to have
a severe breakthrough.

Still masking, social distancing, keeping
out of crowds except for a play in Portland,
I'm trying to do my part amid uncertainty.

I left with a sore arm for a few days. None
of my reactions have been severe. I am still in
lock down mostly . Both of us doing well.

New Year's Valley Drives

Snow-melt puddles,
piles of shoveled snow,
clear blue sky,
Cascade and Coast mountains
topped in white, snow slips
down the slopes like glaciers.
Patches of snow in green fields.
The road free of ice and dry.

Saturday we drove north to Salem.
Deliveries to families of daughter
and grandson. Quick transfers,
masked exchanges, careful hugs.

Sunday I practiced driving locally.
I had not driven for over two years.
Our Honda Fit is easy to drive so I
felt comfortable. I wanted to be ready
for husband' upcoming hip surgery
with help for transport and errands.
Family also helping.

We drove around Corvallis for several
hours and discovered many changes.
Many more consolidated housing options.
Attractive designs. Sun-brightened colors.
We will have me practice up until his surgery.
Post-op I need to be ready to assist.
Despite sore knees, shoulder, and shingle eye,
I can do it!

Rural Roads Loop Drive

On a cloudy gray Saturday,
we took a ride through small
towns in the valley.

White small wooden churches,
and schools, many white fences.
Forests and fields line the road,

flocks of migrating birds when
not resting on power lines
eat abundant grass seed.

A smashed skunk still stinky,
and bloody, two lonely horses
in their large, fenced fields.

Some houses have colorful
paint contrasts, porches
with rocking chairs.

We did not get out of the car.
Drive thrus had long lines.
Indoor dining sparse.

The lush green around us,
somehow reassures some things
endure even in troubled times.

As I watch the Winter Olympics'
spectacular staging and amazing
athletes, I feel hope amid COVID.

Drive to Sea and Fudge

On a sunny Saturday near
Valentine's Day we drive
to Newport, then south by
glistening, silver-tipped waves.

We head for Indulge,
a fudge and brownies shop.
We load up on dark fudge,
a pandemic treat and other times.

He heads inside masked and vaxxed,
to buy a box of fudge which I'll
doll out one piece a day for 12 days.
I nibble one on the way home.

The roads to the coast have a
long caravan–strings of cars.
The road back has less traffic
on a very rural landscape.

People stream like lemmings
to the ocean. It resembles
a summer day. The shops open.
The appearance of normalcy.

Driving home, the political signs
are gone. A lonely horse in a large
field, clustered cows and lambs
enjoy the sun and warmth.

The Winter Olympics are wondrous
and enhanced by fudge. The ride
to the sea is refreshing- waves and
salty air. Sweet moments bring hope.

Jade is a Gem

Oregon State-Stanford Women's Gymnastics Meet.
February 25th Gill Coliseum Jade Carey All-Around 39.825
Beavers: 197.225 Stanford 195.050

The last home meet of the season.
We missed previous home meets
by giving away our season tickets, but
I was determined to see Olympian
Jade Carey in person despite COVID risk.

Jade is one of 21 women gymnasts at OSU.
She signed before the Olympics and now
performs before a masked audience. Athletes
wear masks between events. We had front row
seats in the handicapped section. Really close.

I saw the speck of glitter beside her right eye,
the white toenails, the wrapped right ankle. Her
black leotard had orange sparkles around her
neck and silver-white glitter on her chest and arms.
When the light strikes, they glow.

Jade has very pale skin. At 5'1" she is lean
with muscular shoulders and arms. When she
talked to a team mate she held her throat as if
to indicate she had a sore throat. I wondered
if she would compete and relieved when she did

We sat in a cordoned off area on the gym floor
between the bars and floor exercise mat. OSU's
team stood between the two areas much of the time.
Jade wore her blonde hair in a ponytail with a bow
and tight- to- head braids like many of her the teammates.

Tight butts and flattened chests paraded by.
I could see Jade's moles. At times she was about
four feet away. I did not talk to her, but just
cheered her on like the crowd. She chatted with
her team and smiled often — calm confidence.

She was treated congenially by her team, but
not singled out. She was at ease. When performing
she was precise and dazzling. Three events 9.925
or better and a ten on the floor. When she received
a 10, the audience cheered and jumped wildly.

I wish I went to the other home events. Next season
I hope to attend all the meets. May she stay and I
am not deterred. All the gymnasts were impressive,
stunning. I admire their dedication, skill and grace.
Jade shines like the gem she is.

It Was a Windy, Rainy Ride
   Corvallis to Lincoln City to Newport
   February 27, 2022

It was a gusty, stormy ride
to the coast. Waves bashed the shore.
Traffic moderate. Shops open.

Shops with names like Hippy Trip
and The Chocolate Frog. We went
into the latter....masked.

We also went to the Christmas Cottage.
I found three angels which were my quest.
We ate lunch by drive-thru.

Driving to the coast gets us out
of our COVID cage. Things look normal.
Car chains range from 6-12.

With all the turbulence, cocooned
in the car, as the world passes by,
we feel protected, detached.

When we reach the sea, the waves roil,
the wind blasts us to stay in the car.
I welcome a respite from the familiar.

When we returned home we adjust
quickly to the new normal. Outside the window
robins pluck holly berries, oblivious to me.

Drive to the Coast

Despite weather forecast,
the sun shines with some clouds
all day. A dry drive.

Beside the road near Walton,
white litter bags display black, magic
marker faces with frowns.

Two bags say "litter" and "Don't".
Beyond the bags, trash speckles
and dots the roadside.

At the coast in Florence few people
wear masks, but we do. Some stores
require masks for entrance.

Stores with narrow aisles and distracted
customers make navigating with
a wheel chair a challenge.

Most people seem to be smiling
and accommodating. Local artists' wares
are prominent— wood, glass especially.

I find an exquisite juniper angel
to join my collection and a funky
narrow- brimmed cosmic hat.

Though many lunched inside, we
continue with drive-thru. We are still
being COVID cautious.

Actually I like masks in public. I have
some medical and colorful fabric ones.
Some people are more attractive masked?

Interacting remains tentative. When Zoom
meetings meet in person, will we be masked?
Should I risk a Scrabble game at a home?

I want to protect vulnerable people–especially
our great-grandson, just a year old. Will his
future be masked, filled with fear?

We stay in the car, watch the waves
lap the shore. Things look normal.
When it's warmer I'll resume backyard musings.

Somehow despite restrictions, I'm hopeful
time will wash away our concerns
and we can live more openly.

As Ukraine suffers attacks and the world
seems more fragile again, so far we have
survived, but must we push it forever?

Driving the coast through rural farms
and thriving forest, I can see past litter
bags and rejoice in grazing Black Angus.

Uncertainty and Doubt

Now approaching 82,
there're fewer things I can do.
I rely on grit to get me through.

Too old for hanky-panky.
Constant pain keeps me cranky.
Too often I need a hankie.

COVID lock down still in process.
How long will it progress
until it ends in success?

People bicker and debate
what is to be our fate.
It's hard to communicate.

Strains spread fast, as we slow.
So much we do not know.
How long until grip let's go?

Disconnects, disruptions, fear—
I wonder when emergence will appear
and when an opening will be here.

Reflection and meditation hope to find out
what this situation is all about,
to feel some certainty and confront doubt.

Outdoor Poetry
    Charles Goodrich Poetry reading
    April 10, 2022 Rotary Shelter
    Willamette Park, Corvallis, 3-4 pm.

After over 1000 days. The university and
Grassroots bookstore sponsor a reading outside
with some audience masked and others not.

About sixty people huddle under
the roof, with no sides, sit on
picnic tables and bring their own chairs.

I sit at the edge of a table
near the drips from the roof
during sporadic showers.

It is so cold. Three layers of clothes
are not enough, but most listeners
remain after a long break.

Charles' best older friend of over 40 years,
Clem Starck, 84 introduced him, Both wear
jeans and heavy red and black checker shirts.

Charles reads several poems from
his newest collection "Watering the Rhubarb."
The book is only 42 pages.

I enjoy his nature and political poems
incorporating humor and keen insights–
a poet-gardener.

The intermission was too long. He read
only about six poems after we reassemble.
By then I am very chilled.

My gloves do little to warm me. Despite
the cold, being able to be together as
lock down fades, brings hope.

COVID rules changes for indoors
and outdoors. A gathering of poets
lures other poets and readers.

As I leave, the crowd is too clotted
to penetrate. I cover his book
under my red cape.

The rain pauses en route to the car.
To be outside with poetry, seeing friends–
perhaps soon we'll meet inside together?

Charles, Clem and others belonged
to the same poetry critique group for
decades. Charles was called Chip then.

Now we are all gray and white-haired
with memories of more flamboyant times,
when we lack knowledge of what lies ahead.

Cancelled

We drove to Portland to see
a play at Portland Center Stage,
only to learn the play was cancelled
due to COVID-infected cast members.

We re-booked for mid- June and were
back home by 8:30. This was to be
our first jaunt to a big indoor event
as some pandemic rules loosen.

We would have to wear masks as
we do most everywhere. In our new
car we enjoyed a splendid sunset
and a smooth ride coming back home.

Change comes swiftly. We must
maintain flexibility and a sense of humor.
We had bogged traffic in spots. Still
we were an hour early for the play.

The theater was dark, as we approached
the entry door and we went to the ticket office
to get new tickets. I thought fewer cars
were in the garage than usual.

We had rain and sun en route. It is
a beautiful ride especially in rural areas.
We even bought food from drive-thru,
so this was a car-bound trip.

I feel sorry for the cast. They must
wonder about their safety and pay.
We just had a quicker turn-around.
So much canceled. So much sadness.

A Longer Ride

On our Sunday ride
we drive south in our
new icy blue electric
car we named Ellie.

By field, forests, farms
and small towns, with
sun and rain and sometimes
both at the same time.

We played classical music
and stayed away from the news
of Uvalde's mass shooting and
fear copycat shooters.

Oregon has many shades of green
with outbursts of yellow Scotch broom.
Cattle and sheep graze. All
appears well and normal.

But I can't escape the images
and thoughts about the children
slaughtered by an 18 year old
in Texas. Beyond sad.

We have the most deranged shooters
in the world. What civilian needs an assault rifle?
Let them rent one at shooting galleries. Keep
guns away from deranged people. Beyond sad.

We are already dealing with a pandemic
and our small children cannot be vaccinated.
I worry about my family and the vulnerable
ones around the world. Beyond sad.

Spring tries to cheer me up. Oregon is so
beautiful. But when we drive by an elementary
school I want to cry, worry about our future.
How can we save our children? Beyond sad.

Ride the Mustang

We drive to the coast in our
new icy blue Mustang
with glass, sun protection roof.

Misty, light rain, sun-gaps
through forests, farms
and small towns sprinkle the windshield.

The road is rimmed with white,
yellow and lavender floral patches.
So many shades of green!

As he revels in his new car, I watch
the colorful sentinels as we pass by.
Raindrops dance on the windshield.

We are going to the coast for
dark chocolate fudge and angels.
We came home with fudge.

The ocean rumbles on the shore,
lacy on the beach. We do not stop,
until the fudge shop. We skip angels.

Most people do not wear masks...
but we do. We had a recent surge.
Boosted people still get COVID.

I am at the edge, looking on. I plug
away at poems for a new book as
last one gets illustrated.

The beautiful Mustang is a smooth
ride. As the scenery rolls by, I wish
I felt safe to walk on a green path.

Traveling with Ellie

Ellie is the nickname for Electra,
our 2022, icy blue Ford Mustang.
She is sleek, has comfy interior,
and a display screen which has
access to music, data, programs
routes, just a magician.

I do not dare drive her yet, but
my husband adores her and gladly
drives on our weekend drives—
today to Newport and then north
to Lincoln City and the Christmas Cottage.

When we arrived at the shop where
I hoped to find angels and a witch for a friend.
Then we realized we forgot to load
the walker and wheelchair from the Fit.
We did not get out of the car.

We grabbed fast food and began our trek
home. Daisies, dandelions, lavender lupin,
and other wild flowers line the road— mostly
rural farms and forest. Clear white signs
which Ellie reads, but not yellow signs.
Ellie slows when she knows she should.

A visitor came over soon afterwards, so
it was lucky we came back when we did. He is
a shaman who wanted to consult Court
about an electric water heater. All the house
has been changed to electric power. I
was always afraid of leaking gas.

We can charge Ellie in the garage and I
feel safer. I do not miss smell of gas.
She is not bulbous as hubby called her.
Graceful, generous curves I'd say. As
probably our last car, we both love her.
but I'll still drive the Fit for awhile.

Roadside Haiku
    Images from ride from Corvallis to the coast and back

small birds sit and flit
in the center of the road, dash toward car
but miss our windshield

wild flowers line road
daisies, dandelions, lupin—
nod as we pass by

low tide exposes
rotting logs, decay— hurry
cover up, high tide

rocky road gravel
jars my sore knees, makes Ellie's
smooth ride bumpier

asphalt most of trip
as we take less traveled road
home to recharge car

bunchy, puffy clouds
with blue breezy sky—some shade
in forest places

the world feels safe, calm—
pandemic thoughts set aside
we love Oregon

Heat Wave

Most of the nation is roasting
with a heat wave that covers
much of the country. So far
Oregon is in 80's. 90's next week.

The sun bakes the ground.
Green of all types dries.
I hate to drive to add
to the stagnant pollution.

Going to exercise class,
cars still scurried about
like tiny bugs over the asphalt.
Car windows open and closed.

Waiting in the fast food line,
became suffocating. I almost
left the turgid line for home.
I ordered a large iced diet Coke.

The wind chimes jangle
outside my window as I type.
I want to sit outside and witness
the backyard in action.

But I'll stay inside and peer
outside large windows
and breathe deep cooled air.
I'll wait for a balmier day.

To the Sea and Beyond

On our Saturday ride to the coast,
the forest-lined, rural roads, glisten
in the sun under puffy clouds.

The traffic was light for a mid-August
weekend day. First stop The Christmas
shop where I found three angels.

I decided to be good and not get
fudge next door. I wish I had.
It will be a long fudge-less week.

At the Summit Craft Fair we discovered
mostly food and jewelry. A small holly
bowl about individual salad-size lured me.

Holly wood is very light and creamy with
mostly gray streams flowing through it.
I bought one to admire. I am masked.

Art pierces color into any room. Brightens
tamped pandemic moods. The sea flows,
colors flow, art flows, imagination flows.

I return to the polluted valley, work inside
as the heat wave flows outside. It is not
too hot to sit outside, but I want to cocoon.

Ride to the Sea
Sunday August 28, 2022

We take a Sunday ride to Walport.
It is such a sunny, 70ish day.
The drive to the coast is foresty—
most of the way.

We head south toward Walport
from Newport. We have driven
this route hundreds of times and
each time I discover something
I missed and wonder why.

Today no deer crossed our path.
I was hoping we would see the graceful
gait of a deer as we often do. For me
this is a ride for healing, to be grateful
for such a lovely day.

Yesterday was 40 years since our son
was killed in Tuscaloosa, Alabama. He
was recently 19 and his golden new bike
was crushed also by a man who had killed
others we learned.

Someone taped the event of the accident.
The tape is missing from the shelf. We
have been looking for and trying to find
the tape his parents have not seen, but
other family have and it is missing.

My husband does not want to see it. I am
not sure I do either, but I want to know where
the tape is and who has misplaced it. My
prime suspect said she put it back. She told
me what she remembers seeing.

 I am left bereft, scrambling for firm ground,
typing with heavy fingers with a sad-laden
heart. I still tear up unexpectantly. Perhaps
I should consult a psychic friend for updates?
For now I bear the grief, try to remember–softly.

To the Sea

We try to go to the coast most weekends.
The sea foam on the shore. The sun
shining on the waves. Feet shifting sand.

But I go mostly in search of angels
in very special shops where I always
find a new angel to bring home.

Over 3000 angels in many media
dangle from the walls, line up on
shelves, benches, tables–anywhere.

I relish the wing styles, the inventive
garments, the variety of facial expressions.
They lift me up. My husband shrugs.

For me I can glance at them while
I watch TV, surrounding me. Whatever
is outside, I feel safe inside.

With the pandemic we are still masked
in the shops where new discoveries await.
This weekend we went to near Lincoln City.

The Christmas Cottage has angels all year.
The owner proudly showed me her newest
angels. She know what I am shopping for.

I went home with five. They assumed their
places in the collection. My husband was
doubtful as usual–for me I never doubt angels.

Dark November

With so many people ill,
people afraid to be in public,
wanting to help but feel helpless—
the fall months are dark and sad.

Holidays approach, but many postpone
larger group meetings. Not everyone
has been vaccinated, especially children.

How long does a vaccine protect?
Halloween masks are welcome.
But what about Thanksgiving, Christmas?

I do not dare to host meetings.
I will stay on Zoom for awhile.
Small groups of family might work.

Everything looks so normal. We are
in rainy season as normal. Trees
drip. Shiny holly berries lure birds.

I feel lethargic. I feel the chill
in a heated house and in a sweatshirt.
Artificial light aids my tasks.

Newspapers and tv portray what
we are dealing with–accurately?
Locally we are still limited.

I love the mask designs that pop up
among the medical blue or white masks.
I do not like black masks–too funereal.

I am fortunate we take a weekend drive,
I still go to exercise classes twice a week.
A Friday massage releases toxicity.
Despite maladies, discomfort–I prevail.

Traveling to San Clemente

Twenty hours drive from Corvallis
to San Clemente for a funeral
of my husband's fraternity brother, to
share sadness and support for the family.

It was an Episcopal service with the pastor
in his fancy white embroidered robes
and smug spiritual smile throwing
blessed water on his ashes.

This pomp and ceremony was not
comforting to me, but the tributes
from his friends and family
were very touching.

The photos in the program were
a treasured collection of memories.
It brought back memories of going
to church with my future Episcopalian husband.

We sang hymns whose words were
not ones I believed in. Some Bible passages
were just a bit too much for me to swallow.
I did not take communion. 60+years drought.

I hope all this ritual promotes healing
for his family and friends–all those
who will miss this devout and kind man.
I do believe in hope for recovery.

OTHER BOOKS BY LINDA VARSELL SMITH

Cinqueries: A Cluster of Cinquos and Lanternes
Fibs and Other Truths
Black Stars on a White Sky
Poems That Count
Poems That Count Too
*Winging-It: New and Selected Poems
*Star Stuff: A Soul-Splinter Experiences the Cosmos
*Light-Headed: A Soul-Splinter Experiences Light
*Sparks: A Soul-Splinter Experiences the Earth
*Into the Clouds: Seeking Silver Linings
*Mirabilia: Manifesting Marvels, Miracles and Mysteries
*Spiral Hands: Signs of Healing
*Lacunae: Mind The Gap
*Wayfinding: Navigating the Unknown
*Hugger-Muggery: Ways to Hugs and Mugs
*The Ground Crew: Beings with Earthly Experiences
*Waves: Ebbs and Flows
*Grounded with Gaia: Bonded with Earth
*Changes in Climate: Cleaning the Atmosphere
*Beyond Windows: 2020 Aperatures
*Curves: Swerving Second Half of 2020
*Angels Encore: An Anthology of Angel Poems
*Through Darkness Lightly: Entering 2021
          *Available at www.Lulu.com/spotlight/rainbowcom

Chapbooks: Being Cosmic; Light-headed; Intra-space Chronicles, Red Cape Capers

On-line Website Books: free access Rainbow Communications.org
Syllables of Velvet, Word-Playful, Poetluck

Anthologies: Poets Ponder Photographs; Poetic License; Poet License 2015; The Second Genesis, Jubilee, The Eloquent Umbrella

Twelve novels in the Rainbow Chronicle Series